THE GRAYWOLF

SHORT FICTION SERIES

1 9 8 5

THE GRAYWOLF ANNUAL: SHORT STORIES

EDITED BY SCOTT WALKER

GRAYWOLF PRESS

PORT TOWNSEND

1 9 8 5

Some of the stories collected in *The Graywolf Annual* appeared previously in publications, as noted below. We gratefully acknowledge the cooperation of editors, agents, and the authors.

Daniel Menaker's "Brothers" was first published in *Grand Street*. Copyright © 1982 by Daniel Menaker.

Alice Adams's "Time in Santa Fe" was published in *Fiction Network* (Issue 2). Copyright © 1983 by Alice Adams.

Francis Phelan's "The Battle of Boiling Water" appeared in *The University of Windsor Review*. The story is part of his novel, *Four Ways of Computing Midnight,* due in Spring, 1985, from Atheneum. Copyright © 1979 by Francis Phelan.

Andre Dubus's "After the Game" was published in *Fiction Network*. Copyright © 1983 by Andre Dubus.

Richard Ford's "Winterkill" appeared first in *Esquire*. Copyright © 1983 by Richard Ford.

Elizabeth Cox's "A Sounding Brass" was published in *Antaeus*. Copyright © 1983 by Elizabeth Cox.

Richard DeMarinis's "Under the Wheat" appeared first in *The Iowa Review*. Copyright © 1982 by Rick DeMarinis.

Margaret Atwood's "Simmering" is part of her collection, *Murder in the Dark,* published by Coach House Press (Toronto). Copyright © 1983 by Margaret Atwood.

Tobias Wolff's "Our Story Begins" appeared first in *Esquire*. Copyright © 1984 by Tobias Wolff.

Bobbie Ann Mason's "Hunktown" was published first in *The Atlantic Monthly*. Copyright © 1984 by Bobbie Ann Mason.

The editor is grateful to Raymond Carver, Amanda Urban, and Adrianne Harun for advice, encouragement, and assistance.

Publication of this volume is made possible in part by a grant from the National Endowment for the Arts.

ISBN 0-915308-66-5 / ISSN 0743-7471

Designed by Tree Swenson
Sabon type set by Typeworks, Vancouver
Manufactured by Thomson-Shore

Published by Graywolf Press, Post Office Box 142,
Port Townsend, Washington 98368.

THE GRAYWOLF SHORT FICTION SERIES

Contents

ELIZABETH TALLENT
Half a Mussel Shell

3

ANDRE DUBUS
After the Game

15

DANIEL MENAKER
Brothers

25

ALICE ADAMS
Time in Santa Fe

45

FRANCIS PHELAN
The Battle of Boiling Water

55

RICHARD FORD
Winterkill

71

ELLEN GILCHRIST
The Young Man

93

ELIZABETH COX
A Sounding Brass

103

RICK DEMARINIS
Under the Wheat

119

MARGARET ATWOOD
Simmering

133

TOBIAS WOLFF
Our Story Begins

137

BOBBIE ANN MASON
Hunktown

153

THE GRAYWOLF ANNUAL:

SHORT STORIES

1 9 8 5

ELIZABETH TALLENT

Half a Mussel Shell

A DRAGONFLY drops from thin air, fast as a spider down a thread, and lands on the rim of the teacup in the grass. It rests for an instant, flicking its wings, before contorting itself into a slim, iridescent hairpin, the end of its segmented tail almost touching the miniature gas mask of its face. A ewe lifts its nose from the grass, still chewing, and turns one pale eye on the dragonfly balanced on the cup. Alfred is watching, too, from the porch of the country house where he is sitting cross-legged, the Yeats open on his knee. He feels slightly absurd, watching intently the same thing that the ewe is watching, intently for a sheep: it's like finding you're being followed by a mime.

A second dragonfly circles, flirts with the teacup, and alights. It sidles around and straddles the first, seizing the thorax, Alfred thinks, *with its hands.* He shakes his head at himself, but there is something human in the mounting, avid and comic. At the second dragonfly's weight, the first seems to surrender completely. The upper one dips its tail eagerly, repeatedly, at the tail of the lower, the way a licked thread is aimed at a needle's eye.

"You should come out here, Lisa," Alfred calls. "This is good."

He hears her bare feet on the planks of the porch behind him, and then a finger feathers through his hair, two fingers, the flat of her hand. He reaches backward to catch her wrist, but she's gone.

"What's good?" she says.

He points to the cup, where the dragonflys are glued together. She wrinkles her nose.

"You expect me to drink out of that again?" she says. She sits beside him and taps the page he's been reading, leaving dimples of wet ringed with baby oil. She has been taking a bath.

"I hate this, you know," she says. "A swan can't pick a woman up in his beak. It's like a Road Runner cartoon. He could catch her hair in his beak and twist her neck around and pin her to the ground that way."

"Graphic."

"Well, it would work."

"'But how can body, laid in that white rush,/But feel the strange heart beating where it lies,'" Alfred says. "That's what you hate."

"I'd like to get laid in a white rush, maybe, though."

"You would."

Chin on her knees, she looks at him; he looks back at her. Blond hair drawn into a knot that is a shade darker at the nape, and stray hairs near her face, so blond they're white. He doesn't think she has any actual gray hairs yet. A moth-wing pattern of freckles opening outward from her nose, freckles down her cheekbones and on the upper lip of her solemn, rather wide mouth. In Mexico, where they went to celebrate her month-old divorce, she had a stubborn cold sore inside her lower lip, and the doctor told her it was the sun, simply too much sun: she must, from now on, stay out of the sun. "Then what's the point of being in Mexico?" she asked Alfred, late that night, in their hotel room, as they lay on a bedspread brilliant with birds and leaves. "You could marry me," he said carefully. She turned, her small breast dipping to rest against the wing of a red macaw, and said, "Really?" "Surprise," he said. "You should have told me you had that in mind," she said. "I didn't have it in mind." "You didn't?" "No," he said. "You mean you didn't think of it when I got divorced?" "You needed time," he said. "That's a crock." "Lisa, it's exactly what you would have told me." "You're sure?" "Yes." She moved closer to him, her body hiding a flight of parakeets. "Then yes," she said. "Surprise, yourself."

She scratches her scabbed ankle and then, seriously, begins to pick. She cut the ankle at the beach when he tackled her too hard and she fell, sheltering the football between her breasts, slick in the wet swimsuit. He tugged down the swimsuit strap, pushed the football out of the way, noticing how the goosepimpled aureole seemed drier than the skin around it, and whispered, "Don't leave me." "We've been married a *week*," she said, and they had—after Mexico, they had flown to San Diego, rented a car, and driven north to Bodega, to this house, which was lent to Alfred by his ex-lover, Alexandra. It is a handsome old ranch house with gingerbread below the porch eaves, and unpruned roses that shed flakes of white into the grass of the yard where the landlord's sheep come to graze. Alfred had almost forgotten how much he likes this part of California.

"Leave the scab alone," he says.

"Kiss it."

"No."

"Is this a honeymoon or not?"

"I thought you hated the word."

"I do hate it." She has drawn blood. She looks at her fingernail with satisfaction, begins to draw it along a plank of the porch, and then, turning, wipes it down the page of his book. "I hate it," she says. "I just use it because it turns you on."

"You know the funny thing," he says. "Your blood isn't really very bright."

She has a habit of bringing things into the bed, and it annoys him. He is always kicking or tipping something over in his sleep. Right now, when he turns on his side, he sees her hat with the ribbons and the wide brim in the bed between them. He winds a ribbon around his finger and looks to see if she is smiling. She's not. She's sitting up, holding a metal cigarette box, naked. She clicks the cigarette box open, and he sees tiny spools of thread.

She chooses a shade of thread that matches the ribbon, which matches her hair. She threads a needle and begins to sew the ribbon back on, punching the needle through straw. She looks at him and then she looks down into her lap, pulls the hat onto her knee, and licks her lips.

"You knew that would hurt me, didn't you?"

"What would hurt you, love?" His head feels wooden. Too much sun in the afternoon—he'd forgotten that the California sun can be as hard as Mexico's.

"When you said that."

"Said what?"

"Said my blood wasn't bright."

"Each drop is a garnet." He kisses her foot. "Each drop a ruby."

"You're not awake."

"What time is it?"

"Evening."

"Evening is a time?" He rolls over onto his back and closes his eyes. "I like watching you do that," he says. "But I'm too tired. You pretend I'm watching you."

Later, how much later he can't tell, she wakes him and says, "You can look now."

In dusk, the walls of the room are a warm brown he remembers, a shade Balthus used for some of his backgrounds—not a color anyone could ever deliberately paint a bedroom, but an accidental brown of coastal light slanting along faded wallpaper. He is glad that Alexandra didn't paint it over. She had known that he'd loved the color, and he would have guessed that it would be one of the first things she would change after he left her, five years ago. He had expected her to be vengeful about details, and instead she has left little jokes for him, he supposes for him, throughout the house—in the kitchen a glass that shows Mickey Mouse courting Minnie with a handful of daisies, on the rim of the bathtub a prickly starfish, light as a piece of toast. Once, during a fight in which Alexandra kept stalking naked away from the bed and returning to it, Alfred, lying naked on his side, had counted all the roses on the walls, a sum he's forgotten, though, like her lover's telephone number, it had stayed with him an oddly long time. The number was on a slip of paper in her VISA card's plastic sheath. He had wanted to order a pair of boots from L.L. Bean, and that was how he discovered that she had a lover. He had dialed the number and when the man answered, Alfred knew from the delighted, private way he said "Hello" that he had been counting on the call, and he said, "She isn't going to call you tonight, fucker," and he went upstairs and Alexandra asked, "Who was that you called?" and he said, "Nobody I know," and tossed her wallet on the bed. "But somebody you know, right?" She sat down on the bed and tucked her VISA card back into its sheath and said, "You won't believe this, but this is a relief, in a way."

That was five years ago, and he still expects to come down the stairs and find, first thing, the dumpy old armchair with the lion-claw feet, three feet clasping dirty glass balls and the fourth resting on the floor, its empty mahogany grasp strangely gentle: the armchair where he first read Frank O'Connor's short stories; where he read that saddest of all lives, Hingley's biography of Chekhov; where he read for the first time, for Christ's sake, *Lolita*. He had written a lot of his dissertation in that chair, scribbling in a spiral-ringed notebook propped open on the velvet arm, California light on the page. The armchair is in Boulder now, at the foot of his bed, the bed he slept in with Lisa while she was still married, and slept in alone, whenever he slept, while she and her husband attempted a reconciliation. For two weeks, then three, his silent telephone was always within reach, and then he and Lisa made triumphant, sweaty love in the dead of the Boulder winter, because she had decided to leave her husband "once and for all"—hearing the phrase, Alfred had his first moment of pity for the man. The armchair watched from the end of the bed, shabby and concerned as a fairy-tale bear who'd caught them there, one who was afraid to disturb them but who wanted his bed back.

Nonetheless it is strange to be in this room with Lisa, strange that it is Lisa who is displaying her body against the brown wall, her arms lifted, naked except for the pale hat. He has a pleasant sensation of being unfaithful, so he closes her eyes and tells her apologetically, "It looks wonderful."

There was one obligation Alexandra bestowed on him, along with the tarnished housekey, when they met in the Boulder coffee shop, Alfred between classes, she well into the drive from California to the duplex she'd found, through an ad in the *New York Review of Books,* in Manhattan.

"We always used to do favors for each other, didn't we?" she said. "Isn't this a pretty big favor, letting you stay in my house?"

"It used to be my house, too."

"Half the world once belonged to Spain, Alfred. Half to Portugal."

"Tell me the favor."

Alexandra's black hair was Japanese straight, the fingernails tapping against her espresso cup were glossy ovals—so she no longer chews them to the quick. He had had to snap "Don't," whenever they entered a roomful of people, or she would automatically tuck a fingertip between her teeth, unself-conscious as a cowboy lodging a butt there. She waved away the smoke from the cigarette of a student in the booth behind her, leaned forward, and said, "There's this beautiful elderly bachelor who lives down the road. He bought his house, let's see, the spring after you left, so you never met him. He's alone nearly all the time. His family, what he has left, lives on the East Coast. I want you to ask him over for dinner."

Alfred, who hates to hear men described as "beautiful," a thing women seem to be doing more and more often, said, "Why should I ask him to dinner?"

"He's not any trouble. He's charming."

"A dinner party. I'm not a good cook."

"Dinner party," she scoffed. "You and he."

"I thought I might take someone with me to the house."

"You *might* take someone with you." There it was, the habit as bad as biting her nails when she was upset, she mimicked him. He was never sure whether it was an attempt at irony or a way of stalling for time.

"There's a woman I'm going to Mexico with."

"Yes?"

"And I thought we might drive up along the coast, you know, to the house."

"My house."

"She's nice," he said. "You'd like her."

"I'd *like* her."

"So who is he then, this old guy you want us to ask to dinner?"

"He's an old left-wing journalist. He's been around the world. He saw Hemingway off to Spain to fight. His name is Spencer. He's witty in the way that men used to be witty, without hurting anyone."

"Meaning I've hurt you," Alfred said. "By wanting to take someone with me to the house. It's been a long time, you know. You could have seen something like this coming."

"You know what I think?" she said. "I think there's only one person in the relationship who ever sees things coming, the other one never does. You know what else I think? I think that no matter how long you're apart, that doesn't change. Can she cook?"

"Who?"

"Your lady friend," she mocked him. "Who."

Lisa is asleep on the wicker sofa on the porch when Spencer wheels his bicycle up the long dirt road to the house. Alfred realizes at once that Spencer should never have been termed "an elderly bachelor." His legs are roundly muscled below the ragged running shorts; there is none of that elderly spindliness. He lifts the bicycle across the picket fence around the yard as if it weighed nothing at all.

"Hello," Spencer says. Then he stops, balancing the bicycle by its seat. "I shouldn't have done that," he says. "It's a habit. I'm afraid it looks wrong."

"Leave the bicycle there," Alfred says. "Come on up."

But Spencer stays where he is. "Your wife?"

"Of two weeks," Alfred says. "You're the first person we've seen, except for us." He nudges Lisa with his elbow, which rests along the sofa. In her sleep, her forehead creases.

"She's quite lovely."

Next to hearing men called *beautiful,* Alfred most hates to hear women called *lovely.* "She is," he agrees.

"I came to see about our dinner. I gather you've inherited me from Alexandra?"

Alfred understands he has only to give the slightest hint of resignation or boredom, and the dinner will be impossible because of some sudden obligation of Spencer's. He is tempted to take the opening. He understands that it is a graceful one, yet he dislikes this man so much, on sight, that even his tact is irritating. "In a way, we have," Alfred says.

"Yes?"

"Yes," Alfred says, feeling obscurely bullied. Alexandra likes this man?

"Is Sunday good?"

"Sunday's good."

"I think I'll spend the morning musselling and see if I can't come up with something for our supper."

"You don't have to go to so much trouble."

"They're very good mussels."

"I haven't had them in such a long time."

"Your pretty wife has slept through it," Spencer says. "Does she like mussels?"

"So she has," Alfred says, and "I've no idea. We live in Colorado."

Spencer retrieves his bicycle, lifting it lightly, and straddles it, rising on the toes of his running shoes. When he is a little way down the road, he waves without looking back and calls, "Sunday?"

"Sunday," Alfred echoes.

"What?" Lisa says, sleepily. "What, Sunday?"

"Nothing."

"Come on."

"You're asleep," he says, and smoothes the hair from her forehead.

In a dress that leaves her shoulders bare, her hair knotted at the nape of her neck, which, in candlelight, shows a dim sheen of baby oil incompletely showered away, Lisa is shredding a napkin into her lap.

"It's nice to see what you look like, awake," Spencer says.

"What?"

"You were Sleeping Beauty to my dwarf the first time Spencer appeared," Alfred says.

"Appeared," Spencer says, amused.

"Dwarf," Lisa says. "You're funny tonight."

"You're beautiful tonight," Alfred tells her. "You've completely destroyed your napkin. Your lap is confetti."

She lifts her hand and lets a bit of paper fall. It catches in a candleflame and floats, sparking, onto her plate. "Did you see that?" she says. "That was very strange. I couldn't do it again if I tried." She dips a finger into her waterglass and rubs a dirty streak of ash across her plate.

"Your manners, my dear," Spencer says. In candlelight the planes of his face have a fractured look, the cheeks sharply incised with squint lines below the dark, deeply socketed eyes. His ears are enormous. To Alfred, they have a foxlike look of permanent receptiveness, accentuated by the tuft of silver hair in each interior. Spencer scoops a heap of mussels from a steaming pot onto Lisa's plate. "Salad too," he says, and forks salad from a wooden bowl for her, and then for Alfred. Spencer grinds the pepper mill into the air above her plate. "Say when," he says.

"When," she says.

"Just like a good waiter," Alfred says.

"I am a good waiter," Spencer says.

"Thank you," Lisa says; the tines of her fork pierce a curved shard of tomato.

"From the Farmer's Market," Spencer says, watching her.

"Tell me about Spain during the war," Alfred says. "When you were with Hemingway."

"I wasn't *with* Hemingway. I saw him off."

"You saw him off. At the dock, you mean."

Lisa slips a mussel from her plate. Alfred sees this from the corner of his eye. Then he feels the mussel slide into his lap, a wet oval stone. He presses his thighs together so it won't fall.

"Hemingway was always in love with his first wife, Hadley," Spencer says. "Or he always believed that he was, which comes to the same thing. When he left his second wife, Pauline, whom he believed had stolen him from Hadley, he said a cruel thing. He said, 'Those who live by the sword shall die by the sword.'"

"He was wrong," Alfred says. "He was wrong to blame

Pauline for something he did." Another mussel shell tips into his lap. It makes a small click as it settles against the first. The dampness seeps into his Levi's. He looks at Lisa, but she refuses to catch his eye.

"It's natural," she says, "to blame someone else for something you wanted to do. What could be more human?" She takes half a shell and examines it—the black-purple shell, sleek and dimpled as an eel's skin, the interior sharply salmon pink, grained with an iridescence that brightens as she holds the shell above a candle flame. "It's probably too hard to accept the things we do, otherwise."

"This is the part I like," Spencer says. He is digging delicately at a nugget of mussel; Alfred hears the tines of his fork scrape the shell. Spencer glances up at Lisa and his teeth show, white. "The trouble it was getting these is worth it, if you like them."

"They're very good," she says. "I can't think of anything I would rather have had for dinner." Her shoulders gleam as she leans across the table to touch Spencer's hand, the hand holding the fork, the fork scraping the shell, while the black mussels cool slowly in Alfred's lap.

"Say you'll stay," Alfred says. He rests his wineglass on the splintered porch railing.

"I can't, really," Spencer says. "The bicycle hasn't got any lights, and it isn't safe on the road after dusk without them."

Alfred hates the way he says *dusk* instead of *dark*. Spencer strokes the bicycle's handlebars. "I don't know why I never remembered to get lights."

"Please come back," Alfred says. "Come back soon."

"Very soon," Lisa says. "We were getting lonely."

"I'd like that, in fact."

"You know, the padlock on the bridge gate is tricky," Lisa says. "It's hard to work it right, in the dark. Would you like me to come with you?"

"I can manage," Spencer says. "I've come this way a hundred times."

"I need the walk, after a dinner like that," Lisa says.

"You need the walk. Then by all means."

"Don't get lost," Alfred says.

"We won't," Lisa says.

Spencer walks with the bicycle leaning lightly against his thigh. His running shorts seem ridiculously brief, now that the evening has begun to turn cool; his long legs have an exposed look. The center ridge of the dirt road separates him from Lisa, reeds and foxtails flicking forward, drawn into the bicycle's spokes. Alfred listens to the bicycle's ticking until they disappear around a curve in the road. The moon is rising above a ridge. He settles back into the wicker sofa with his book and his glass of wine. It is a half mile walk to the gate. He turns the pages of the Yeats, and when a mosquito lights on the first line of "Nineteen Hundred and Nineteen," he crushes it with his thumb. It makes a sooty smudge, the legs, still intact, long as a cat's whiskers, but helplessly askew. He wonders whose the bright blood is.

ANDRE DUBUS

After the Game

I WASN'T in the clubhouse when Joaquin Quintana went crazy. At least I wasn't there for the start of it, because I pitched that night and went nine innings and won, and the color man interviewed me after the game. He is Duke Simpson and last year he was our first baseman. He came down from the broadcasting booth, and while the guys were going into the clubhouse, and cops and ushers were standing like soldiers in a V from first to third, facing the crowd leaving the park, I stood in front of the dugout with my jacket on, and Duke and I looked at the camera, and he said: "I'm here with Billy Wells."

This was August and we were still in it, four games back, one and a half out of second. It was the time of year when everybody is tired and a lot are hurt and playing anyway. I wanted a shower and a beer, and to go to my apartment for one more beer and then sleep. I sleep very well after I've pitched a good game, not so well after a bad one, and I sleep very badly the night before I pitch, and the day of the game I force myself to eat. It's one of the things that makes the game exciting, but a lot of times, especially in late season, I long for the time when I'll have a job I can predict, can wake up on the ranch knowing what I'm going to do, and that I'm not going to fail. I know most jobs are like that, and the people who have them don't look like they've had a rush of adrenaline since the time somebody ran a stop sign and just missed colliding broadside with them, but there's always a trade-off and, on some days in late season, their lives seem worth it. Duke and I talked about pitching, and our catcher Jesse Wade and what a good game he called behind the plate, so later that night I thought it was strange, that Joaquin was going crazy while Duke and I were talking about Jesse, because during the winter the club had traded Manuel Fernandez, a good relief pitcher, to the Yankees for Jesse. Manuel had been Joaquin's roommate, and they always sat together on the plane and the bus, and ate together. Neither one could speak much English. From shortstop, Joaquin used to call to Manuel out on the mound: *Bajo y rapido.*

We ended the interview shaking hands and patting each other on the back, then I went between the cops and ushers but there were some fans waiting for autographs at one end of the dugout, so I went over there and signed three baseballs and a dozen scorecards and said thank you twenty or thirty times, and shook it seemed more hands than there were people, and then went into the dugout and down the tunnel to the clubhouse. I knew something was wrong, but I wasn't alert to it, wanting a beer, and I was thinking maybe I'd put my arm in ice for a while, so I saw as if out of the corner of my eye, though I was looking right at it, that nobody was at the food table. There was pizza. Then I heard them and looked that way, down between two rows of lockers. They were bunched down there, the ones on the outside standing on benches or on tiptoes on the floor, stretching and looking, and the ones on the inside talking, not to each other but to whoever was in the middle, and I could hear the manager Bobby Drew and Terry Morgan, the trainer. The guys' voices were low, so I couldn't make out the words, and urgent, so I wondered who had been fighting and why now, with things going well for us, and we hadn't had trouble on the club since Duke retired; he was a good ballplayer, but often a pain in the ass. I went to the back of the crowd but couldn't see, so took off my spikes and stepped behind Bruce Green on a bench. Bruce is the only black on the club, and plays right field. I held his waist for balance as I brought my other foot from the floor. I stay in good running shape all year round, and I am overly careful about accidents, like falling off a bench onto my pitching elbow.

I kept my hands on Bruce's waist and looked over his shoulder and there was Joaquin Quintana, our shortstop, standing in front of his locker, naked except for his sweat socks and jock strap and his gold Catholic medal, breathing through his mouth like he was in the middle of a sentence he didn't finish. He was as black as Bruce, so people who didn't know him took him for a black man, but Manuel told us he was from the Dominican Republic and did not think of himself as black, and was pissed off when people did; though it seemed to me he was a black from down there, as Bruce was a black from Newark. His left arm was at his side, and his right forearm was out in front of him like he was reaching for something, or to shake hands, and in that hand he held his spikes. It was the right shoe.

Bruce looked at me over his shoulder.

"They can't move him," he said. Bruce was wearing his uniform pants and no shirt. I came to Boston in 1955, as a minor league player to be named later in a trade with Detroit, when I was in that organization, and I have played all my seven years of major league ball with the Red Sox; I grew up in San Antonio, so Bruce is the only black I've ever really known. People were talking to Joaquin. Or the people in front were trying to, and others farther back called to him to have some pizza, a beer, a shower, telling him it was all right, everything was all right, telling him settle down, be cool, take it easy, the girls are waiting at the parking lot. Nobody was wet or wrapped in a towel. Some still wore the uniform and some, like Bruce, wore parts of it, and a few had taken off as much as Joaquin. Most of the lockers were open. So was Joaquin's, and he stood staring at Bobby Drew and Terry Morgan, both of them talking, and Bobby doing most of it, being the manager. He was talking softly and telling Joaquin to give him the shoe and come in his office and lie down on the couch in there. He kept talking about the shoe, as if it was a weapon, though Joaquin held it with his hand under it, and not gripped for swinging, but like he was holding it out to give to someone. But I knew why Bobby wanted him to put it down. I felt the same: if he would just drop that shoe, things would get better. Looking at the scuffed toe and the soft dusty leather and the laces untied and pulled wider across the tongue folded up and over, and the spikes, silver down at their edges, resting on his palm, I wanted to talk that shoe out of his hand too, and I started talking with the others below me, and on the bench across the aisle from me and Bruce, and the benches on the other side of the group around Joaquin.

That is when I saw what he was staring at, when I told him to come on and put down that shoe and let's go get some dinner, it was on me, and all the drinks too, for turning that double-play in the seventh; and Bruce said And the bunt, and Jesse said Perfect fucking bunt, and I saw that Joaquin was not staring at Bobby or Terry, but at nothing at all, as if he saw something we couldn't, but it was as clear to him as a picture hanging in the air right in front of his face.

I lowered myself off the bench and worked my way through the guys, most of them growing quiet while some still tried to break Joaquin out of it. A few were saying their favorite curse, to themselves, shaking their heads or looking at the floor. Everyone I touched was standing tense and solid, but they were easy to part from each other, like pushing aside branches that smelled of sweat. I stepped between Bobby and Terry. They were still dressed, Bobby in his uniform and cap, Terry in his red slacks and white tee shirt.

Quintana," I said. "Joaquin: it's me, old buddy. It's Billy."

I stared into his eyes but they were not looking back at me; they were looking at something, and they chilled the backs of my knees. I had to stop my hands from going up and feeling the air between us, grabbing for it, pushing it away.

There is something about being naked. Duke Simpson and Tommy Lutring got in a fight last year, in front of Duke's locker, when they had just got out of the shower, and it was not like seeing a fight on the field when the guys are dressed and rolling in the dirt. It seemed worse. Once in a hotel in Chicago a girl and I started fighting in bed and quick enough we were out of bed and putting on our underpants; the madder we got the more clothes we put on, and when she ended the fight by walking out, I was wearing everything but my socks and shoes. I wished Joaquin was dressed.

"Joaquin," I said. "Joaquin, I'm going to take the shoe."

Some of the guys told him to give Billy the shoe. I put my hand on it and he didn't move; then I tried to lift it, and his arm swung a few degrees, but that was all. His bicep was swollen and showing veins.

"Come on, Joaquin. Let it go now. That's a boy."

I put my other hand on it and jerked, and his arm swung and his body swayed and my hands slipped off the shoe. He was staring. I looked at Bobby and Terry, then at the guys on both sides; my eyes met Bruce's, so I said to him: "He doesn't even know I'm here."

"Poor bastard," Bobby said.

Somebody said we ought to carry him to Bobby's couch, and Terry said we couldn't because he was stiff as iron, and lightly, with his fingertips, he jabbed Joaquin's thighs and belly and arms and shoulders, and put his palms on Joaquin's cheeks. Terry said we had to wait for Doc Segura, and Bobby told old Will Hammersley, the clubhouse man, to go tell the press he was sorry but they couldn't come in tonight.

Then we stood waiting. I smelled Joaquin's sweat and listened to his breathing, and looked up and down his good body, and at the medal hanging from his neck, and past his eyes, into his locker: the shaving kit and underwear and socks on the top shelf, with his wallet and gold banded wristwatch and box of cigars. A couple of his silk shirts hung in the locker, one aqua and one maroon, and a sport coat that was pale yellow, near the color of cream; under it some black pants were folded over the hanger. I wondered what it was like being him all the time. I don't know where the Dominican Republic is. I know it's in the Carribean, but not where. Over the voices around me, Tommy Lutring said: "Why the *fuck* did we trade *Manuel?*" Then he said: "Sorry, Jesse."

"I wish he was here," Jesse said.

The guys near Jesse patted him on the shoulders and back. Lutring is the second baseman and he loves working with Joaquin. They are something to see, and I like watching them take infield practice. In a game it happens very fast, and you feel the excitement in the moments it takes Joaquin and Tommy to turn a double-play, and before you can absorb it, the pitcher's ready to throw again. In practice you get to anticipate, and watch them poised for the groundball, then they're moving, one to the bag, one to the ball, and they always know where the other guy is and where his glove is too, because whoever's taking the throw knows it's coming at his chest, leading him across the bag. It is like the movies I used to watch in San Antonio, with one of those dances that start with a chorus of pretty girls, then they move back for the man and woman: he is in a tuxedo and she wears a long white dress that rises from her legs when she whirls. The lights go down on the chorus, and one light moves with the man and woman dancing together and apart but always together. Light sparkles on her dress, and their shadows dance on the polished floor. I was a kid sitting in the dark, and I wanted to dance like that, and felt if I could just step into the music like into a river, the drums and horns would take me, and I would know how to move.

That is why Tommy said what he did. And Jesse said he wished Manuel was here too, which he probably did not really, not at the price of him being back with the Yankees where he was the back-up catcher, while here he is the regular and also has our short left field wall to pull for. Because we couldn't do anything and we started to feel like Spanish was the answer, or the problem, and if just somebody could speak it to Joaquin he'd be all right and he'd put down that shoe and use his eyes again, and take off his jockstrap and socks, and head for the showers, so if only Manuel was with us or one of us had learned Spanish in school.

But the truth is the president or dictator of the Dominican Republic couldn't have talked Joaquin into the showers. Doc Segura gave him three shots before his muscles went limp and he dropped the shoe and collapsed like pants you step out of. We caught him before he hit the floor. The two guys with the ambulance got there after the first shot, and stood on either side of him, behind him so they were out of Doc's way; around the end, before the last shot, they held Joaquin's arms, and when he fell Bobby and I grabbed him too. His eyes were closed. We put him on the stretcher and they covered him up and carried him out and we haven't seen him since, though we get reports on how he's doing in the hospital. He sleeps and they feed him. That was three weeks ago.

Doc Segura had to wait thirty minutes between shots, so the smokers had their cigarettes and cigars going, and guys were passing beers and pizza up from the back, where I had stood with Bruce. He was still on the bench, drinking a beer, with smoke rising past him to the ceiling. I didn't feel right, drinking a beer in front of Joaquin, and I don't think

Bobby did either. Terry is an alcoholic who doesn't drink anymore and goes to meetings, so he didn't count. Finally when someone held a can toward Bobby he didn't shake his head, but got it to his mouth fast while he watched Doc getting the second needle ready, so I reached for one too. Doc swabbed the vein inside Joaquin's left elbow. This time I looked at Joaquin's eyes instead of the needle: he didn't feel it. All my sweat was long since dried, and I had my jacket off except the right sleeve on my arm.

I know Manuel couldn't have helped Joaquin. The guys keep saying it was because he was lonesome. But I think they say that because Joaquin was black and spoke Spanish. And maybe for the same reason an alcoholic who doesn't drink anymore may blame other people's troubles on booze: he's got scary memories of blackouts and sick hangovers and d.t.'s, and he always knows he's just a barstool away from it. I lost a wife in my first year in professional ball, when I was eighteen years old and as dumb about women as I am now. Her name was Leslie. She left me for a married dentist, a guy with kids, in Lafayette, Louisiana, where I was playing my rookie year in the Evangeline League, an old class C league that isn't there anymore. She is back in San Antonio, married to the manager of a department store; she has four kids, and I hardly ever see her, but when I do there are no hard feelings. Leslie said she felt like she was chasing the team bus all season long, down there in Louisiana. I have had girl friends since, but not the kind you marry.

By the time Joaquin fell I'd had a few beers and some pizza gone cold, and I was very tired. It was after one in the morning and I did not feel like I had pitched a game, and won it too. I felt like I had been working all day on the beef cattle ranch my daddy is building up for us with the money I send him every pay day. That's where I'm going when my arm gives out. He has built a house on it, and I'll live there with him and my mom. In the showers people were quiet. They talked, but you know what I mean. I dressed then told

Hammersley I wanted to go into the park for a minute. He said Sure, Billy, and opened the door.

I went up the tunnel to the dugout and stepped onto the grass. It was already damp. I had never seen the park empty at night, and with no lights, and all those empty seats and shadows under the roof over the grandstand, and under the sky the dark seats out in the bleachers in right and center-field. Boston lit the sky over the screen in left and beyond the bleachers, but it was a dull light, and above the playing field there was no light at all, so I could see stars. For a long time until I figured everybody was dressed and gone or leaving and Hammersley was waiting to lock up, I stood on the grass by the batting circle and looked up at the stars, thinking of drums and cymbals and horns, and a man and woman dancing.

Brothers

I

SIMON GREEN was twenty-six. He taught English at a good private boys' school in Manhattan. His brother, Nicholas, was twenty-nine and worked as an associate in a Wall Street law firm.

Nick was darker than Simon, taller, thicker. Simon had a fair complexion and curly straw-colored hair. Nick could fix small things, Simon's handwriting was impatient-looking and crude. Nick told stories, Simon joked. Nick was married, organized, cautious; Simon could listen to the same rock-and-roll song or even just the ending to the same song fifteen times.

On Thanksgiving Day Nick and Simon were playing touch football on the lawn in front of their parents' house, in Palisades, New York. The drab-green lawn stretched from the front of the house to the very edge of the Hudson River, which on this day was chopped into sharp, angry-looking waves by a chilly north wind. The brothers were playing against two rich cousins from Boston, John and Daniel Randolph. Nick's wife, Nancy, looked on as the four young men had their fun. Louise Carter, Simon's girlfriend, stood near the river, her back to the house, her shoulders drawn in against the wind, and gazed over the water. Louise, who was from South Carolina, had been two years behind Simon in college and after she graduated she came to New York to try to be an actress. They were always talking about getting married.

Nick had a bad right knee, so Simon had to play backfield on defense and receiver on offense. He was getting worn out, and finally he said to Nick, "Why don't you play pass defense for once. Your precious knee will hold up." Nick said, O.K., he would. On the next play, John went out for a pass. He and Nick got themselves into a cartoon-like tangle of arms and legs when they went up for the ball. They were both tall and solid, and when they hit the ground, Simon felt a vibration through his feet, as if from an earthquake two hundred miles away. Nick came down with his right leg bent, and he cried out in pain. Nancy ran to where he lay on the ground, grimacing and shaking his head as if he could refuse the injury, and as she rolled up the leg of his jeans, she gave Simon a filthy glare.

"Look at that," she said. "Maybe it's not so bad."

"It's bad enough," Nick said as Nancy poked at his knee. "Jesus, Nance, what are you doing?"

Simon, who had been pacing around fifteen yards away, now walked over to Nick. "Defensive interference," he said.

"That's really funny," Nancy said.

"Help me up, Simple Simon," Nick said. "I can't walk on this thing."

Simon took Nick's hand and hauled him upright. Nick draped his arm over Simon's shoulder. After a few steps, Nick said, "Wait a minute. My leg is freezing." He bent over and rolled down his jeans. Simon looked over the lawn to where Louise was standing, oblivious of what had happened. With her back still to the house, she turned three cartwheels, her long hair streaming out like a black pennant.

Nick was to be operated on in a Brooklyn hospital on the tenth of December by an orthopedic surgeon who was a friend of the family's. Simon had misgivings about the doctor and the hospital but felt that he had already caused enough trouble and kept his mouth shut. The night before the operation, Simon, who had come down with a mild strep throat, called Nick in the hospital. "I'm really sorry about all this," he said, in a raspy voice.

"Oh, you sensitive asshole," Nick said. "Forget about it."

"I shouldn't have made you play backfield."

"The day you make me do anything," Nick said.

"When's the operation?" Simon asked.

"Seven tomorrow morning. I'm sort of scared."

"Don't be ridiculous," Simon said. "It wasn't bad the first time you had it."

"It hurt like a bitch for a whole week afterward. You couldn't have stood it, Mister Delicate. You would have been a real case. The pain, the pain."

"¡Qué lástima!" Simon said. "Did I tell you I was tutoring one of the kids at school in Spanish? P.S., he's Puerto Rican. He speaks street Spanish, and—"

"Wait, here's Nancy. Listen, I'll talk to you tomorrow or the next day. In extreme agony."

"Come on," Simon said. "You'll be O.K."

When Nick Green had married Nancy, two years earlier, Simon felt as if some strange kind of operation had hollowed out part of his body. It was ridiculous, he knew, but he imagined that he could actually locate the site of the loss; it was on his left side, from the inner part of his upper arm, up and under his armpit, and then along his rib cage—a shape like the winning two-thirds of a used wishbone. Simon was Nick's best man at the wedding, which took place at Nancy's parents' big house in Mount Kisco, and only two things went wrong: he forgot to include a shirt with Nick's traveling clothes, so that one of the guests of Nick's size had to lend him his; and during the ceremony Simon felt an ache in his ribs, as if the minister were a juju man working on the marrow of his bones.

The wedding did nothing but further attenuate the bond

between the two brothers, which had already grown thin and tense. From the time that Simon had begun teaching and Nick had started at the law firm and met Nancy, the roughhousing, the sharp sarcasm, the ritual disputes about who was the smarter, the more athletic, the better looking all withered away. When Simon tried to revive them, he almost always ended up feeling stupid and embarrassed, as if he had told a joke that nobody laughed at.

Nick had been born when their mother, Emily, was thirty-seven; Simon, when she was forty. She went back to her job as chief copy editor for an art magazine soon after, leaving them largely in the care of a loving and garrulous black woman. Their father, Joseph, struggled at being an institutional-insurance salesman, traveling throughout South America on business when they were young.

The boys were raised to call their parents Emily and Joe and not to call on God at all. They lived in Greenwich Village and went to a progressive school. Joe was the younger son of two White Russian émigrés. Emily, who came from a wealthy Philadelphia Quaker family, listened patiently to Joe's righteous complaints, indulging him just as she indulged her boys.

Simon grew into adolescence sensing that things in his family were not as they ought to be, and not knowing that they never were in any family. The constant in his life was his brother.

On the day of Nick's operation, Simon's strep throat got worse, and by the time he met the ten seniors in his advanced English class, after lunch, he sounded like a movie monster.

"The last time, we started to talk about 'Ode on a Grecian Urn,'" he croaked, "and I asked each of you to write in a single sentence what you thought Keats was trying to say in it—what its theme was—and to be ready to back it up with evidence from—Tim, put your hand down or you'll lose the circulation in it. We're going to do this in alphabetical order."

"I guess I've got to be prepared to go through the rest of my life like this," Ken Aaron said. "'The Ode on a Grecian Urn' is about a beautiful urn, or large vase, with various paintings on it that show how art is better than real life," Ken said.

"Yes, maybe," Simon said, "but what is 'Ode on a Grecian Urn' about?"

"I just told you, sir," Ken said.

"No, you told us what '*The* Ode on a Grecian Urn' was about. Now, Danny Heisler." Simon got up and started pacing.

" 'Ode on a Grecian Urn' is about time—how you can't live or be happy in it or outside of it."

Simon stopped and squinted at Danny, his favorite. "Didn't I teach your brother Nick—I mean, Mike—this poem two years ago?"

"He's not even home from vacation yet, sir. This is my own idea. You have a suspicious nature, sir."

"Sir, that was my idea, too," Tim Shaffer said.

"That I have a suspicious nature?"

Another teacher came into the room. There was a call for Simon on the public phone on the first floor.

It was his mother calling from the hospital. "Nicky has a blood infection," she said. "He was operated on at seven-thirty this morning, and now he has a temperature of a hundred and five."

Simon said, "O.K., I'll be there as soon as I can."

He hung up and called Louise, and told her what had happened. She said she would go to the hospital, too.

The hospital was way out in Brooklyn, in a neighborhood where the apartment houses were only five or six stories high, on broad gray avenues with too few cars and divided by mean, low concrete islands; the lampposts stuck out like a parade of crane's legs—the only thing that didn't look stepped-on and squashed.

As Simon walked down the hospital's long corridors, he

came upon knots of two, three, four people—doctors and
nurses and perhaps relatives—standing together and
speaking quietly, nodding and inclining toward one
another, heavy with plans. He saw his mother and father
and the surgeon near the end of a long hall, outside Nick's
room. Though she was shorter than the two men, Emily
seemed to dominate them; there was some greater element
of refinement in her bearing, in her mottled, craggy good
looks. Joe stood next to her like a handsome escort. His hair
was white with streaks of black, his nose was large and dis-
tinguished, but his eyes were reservoirs of deference. Joe
draped his arm around Simon's shoulder. Emily tilted her
head so Simon could kiss her on the cheek. The surgeon
clasped Simon's hand with both of his.

"He was delirious for a while," Emily said. "They moved
his roommate out because Nicky was—ranting. They've
used an ice blanket to bring his temperature down. Do you
want to see him?"

"Well, I'm still trying to get over this strep throat," Simon
said.

"Then it might not be a good idea for you to see him," the
surgeon said. "As I was telling your mother and father,
some staph bug must have jumped in there during the
operation, and now your brother has this septicemia."

"How long is it going to go on?" Simon said.

The surgeon explained Nick's condition. He looked relieved when a sound came out of his white coat. "My beep-
er," he said.

His place was taken, almost magically, by Louise and
Nancy, the one girl lovely, with white skin and straight dark
hair, looking the part of the actress she was trying to
become, the other more conventionally pretty, wearing in
the lapel of her tweedy jacket a pin of the logo of the large
charity she worked for. They both had terrified smiles on
their faces. "We came on the same subway," they said in
unison, and everyone laughed loudly.

"Are we allowed to see him?" Nancy said.

Joe and Emily and Simon all said yes. More laughter, then silence, like the kind at a cocktail party following a *faux pas*.

"He's asleep, but it's all right to see him," Emily said.

Simon made Nancy stay out in the hall. "Are you angry at me?" he said.

"Oh, for heaven's sake, why should I be angry at you?" she said.

"Well, you were staring daggers at me after Nicky got hurt, and it was sort of my fault."

"I didn't know you performed the surgery," she said. Then she began to cry. Very tentatively, Simon put his arms around her. "Don't be ridiculous," she said through her tears. "It's not your fault at all."

Simon felt embarrassed holding his brother's wife. Her breasts against him, his hands on her narrow back.

At six, someone suggested that they should find the hospital's cafeteria and go there in two shifts. Simon said wouldn't it be better if he went out to a coffee shop and brought back some food. Louise offered to go with him.

It was cold on the street, and the strong wind drove a sandy, stinging snow down the avenue. Louise said, "Do you remember three summers ago when Nicky was living at home and studying for his bar exam? We went up in Palisades for the weekend and he wanted to go to the beach, but you didn't want to, so I went with him."

"And got a crush on him," Simon said.

"Now how did you know that?"

"Everyone I ever went out with who met Nicky got a crush on him. We both have something that the other lacks, I guess."

"I think he got a little crush on me, too," Louise said.

"Why wouldn't he, two hours in the car and two hours on the beach with you in a bikini?" Simon said.

They passed under a streetlight and stopped at the curb.

"You do realize that we're talking about him as if he were going to die," Simon said.

They found a dreary cafeteria-diner. The man behind the counter said, "Sorry, buddy, I'd like to help you but I don't have take-out." Simon said that his brother was in the hospital down the street, and wasn't there some way of taking something back to his parents? The man said, "Why didn't you say so in the first place? You don't sound so good yourself." He wrapped up some hamburgers and small salads. After they paid for the food, the counterman said, "Your brother is a young man?"

"Twenty-nine," Simon said.

"Then it isn't his heart?"

"No," Simon said. "He got a blood infection after a knee operation. It's called septicemia."

"But he's young, it isn't his heart, he'll be fine," the man said. "Up and around in no time."

"You really think so?" Simon said.

"No question about it."

At eleven that night, Simon and Joe went to the nurses' desk to hire a private nurse for Nick for the midnight shift. "Find a pretty one, like you," Joe said to the floor supervisor, a slender West Indian black woman.

"Mister, that boy could have his pick," he said. "He's got your looks."

As Simon and his father walked away from the nurses' station, Joe said, "I shouldn't have let Nicky come here."

"But it wasn't up to you, was it?" Simon said. "Listen, this is an accident," he went on, sawing the air with his hand in his best classroom manner. "Everyone can find a way to feel responsible if he tries hard enough, but it's no one's fault." He didn't believe a word of it.

"You sound very authoritative," Joe said. "Just like your mother."

They all tried to get some sleep in the lounge. After an hour or so of shifting around in one of the horrible chairs, Simon got up quietly and wandered the hospital's halls. Coming back to the lounge from a new direction, he found two service elevators hidden away in a sort of blind-alley corridor. Outside the elevators was a gurney bed covered with a clean sheet. He took off his sport coat, climbed up onto the bed, and lying on his back, drifted off into a restless sleep.

At dawn, Simon woke and went back to the lounge. Everyone else was still asleep, Emily and Joe on the couches, Louise and Nancy on the floor with chair cushions as makeshift pallets. As Simon was looking at them all, groggily, a resident came up to him.

"My brother?" Simon said.

"He's awake," the resident said. "He's not doing too well but you can see him."

"Well, I've got this strep throat," Simon said.

The doctor, a tall, sallow young man whose arms and legs seemed slightly out of his control, beckoned Simon out into the hall. "This situation will probably continue for a while," he said. "I just wanted to inform you that there's a residence for nurses and doctors across the street. One of the suites there may be available."

"It would be much better," Simon said, glancing back at the lounge.

The resident nodded his head once, sharply. He pivoted on one heel, but as he walked away his arms and legs resumed living their own somewhat wayward lives.

They would all need clean clothes and toothbrushes, and Louise had to go to her apartment in the Village to get ready for a TV-commercial audition. Simon volunteered to take Joe's car and drop Louise off, collect stuff from the house in

Palisades, and then stop at his West Side apartment and Nick and Nancy's on Henry Street. Joe said, "And would you ask the girl next door to keep feeding the damn cats?" He gave Simon the car keys. "It's a good thing I had the snow tires put on the other day," he said. "I'm rather proud of myself."

There was a public phone just down the hall from the cafeteria, and Simon used it to call school, to say that he wouldn't be coming in. He asked for Mr. Anderson, the headmaster. After Simon explained what had happened, Mr. Anderson said something about hoping that things would be all right, and Simon felt so grateful that tears filled his eyes.

II

There was a long silence as Simon and Louise maneuvered through the heavy traffic at the approach to the Brooklyn Bridge. The traffic stopped entirely halfway across the bridge. Manhattan loomed ahead in the mist like a vast, floating fortress. Simon recalled to himself an incident from his childhood in which Nick had offered to beat up some kid who had called him a kike. "Now I guess I'm talking about him the way you were last night," Simon said out loud. He looked over at Louise and saw that she was fast asleep, her head back on the top of the seat, her thick hair falling away from her face like some heavy, fine cloth. He reached across her and took her right hand, which was hanging down beside the seat, and put it on her lap. The traffic started moving again. "The point is," Simon said quietly.

After dropping Louise off, Simon drove to the West Side Highway by a route that took him along Horatio Street, past the house where he lived the first ten years of his life. It was a fine old brownstone, now divided up into apartments: he could see the mailboxes in the vestibule as he drove by.

The big lawn in front of the house in Palisades was dusted over with snow. The sky was becoming lighter, and occasionally the sun shone through and made the Hudson sparkle. Upstairs in the rambling house, Simon, carrying a small suitcase, moved from one room to another feeling like a thief. He stood in his mother's room, looking at the painting given her by an Ashcan artist to repay a loan thirty years before, at the white tufted bedspread that he himself had sent home from his summer tour of Europe, at the two Navajo rugs, at the cherrywood bureau and dressing table, at the books and magazines on the dressing table—William Maxwell's *The Folded Leaf*, Firbank's Life of E. M. Forster, the Wellesley alumnae bulletin—and he thought about the accident of wealth that permitted all this material and emotional refinement, and then about the sophomore's questions of how it was that he was who he was and not someone else, how it had been arranged that it was not he but his brother who now lay near death. Dizziness nearly overcame him, as it had during his mother's first phone call, and he lay down on her bed, the constellation of his family whirling in his head: he was his brother's older brother, his father's father, his mother's husband, his own father.

There were two faint reports from downstairs. Simon wondered for a moment whether someone was knocking on the front door. But then he heard a jumble of small footfalls in the foyer and then on the stairs, like a minuscule stampede, and he knew that the thumps had been the cat door in the basement banging shut twice. The two orange cats came up the stairs and followed Simon to his father's room, in the rear of the house, away from the river, and far enough away from his mother's room to ensure that his snoring would not disturb her. It was a rooming-house room, with brown linoleum on the floor, a camp bed, and a functional desk and chair. The clock on the bed table was an old electric one made of yellowing plastic with a large crack in the casing.

The shoes in a neat row on the floor under the bed were mostly castoffs from Simon that his father had had fixed and then saddle-soaped and polished. Simon went into the bathroom to get his father's toothbrush. There were cobwebs in the corners where the walls met the ceiling.

He walked toward the front of the house again, past Nick's old room, the cats still trailing him. He went downstairs to give them something to eat. On the door to his own bedroom, next to his brother's, was a sign that said "*NO MOLESTE, POR FAVOR,*" which his father had brought back from a hotel in Argentina a long, long time before. Simon obeyed it, leaving undisturbed the shade of the teen-age boy who retreated there so often to escape his brother's ridicule, who so often at night lay sleepless on the narrow bed, who did not know whether he was hero or scoundrel, dirty or clean, weak or tough, smart or devious, who did not even know, because there was no one with the time or inclination to tell him, whether these doubts were unique or vulgar, inborn or reactionary, and who hoarded them like a miser, because they made him feel special, and because he felt that he would be loved to the degree that he caused no trouble. The bright sun in the kitchen cheered him, and he didn't notice the cold as he walked across the driveway and through a gap in the hedge, toward the neighbor's house, to extend the arrangement for feeding the cats.

Back at his parents' house, he picked up the suitcase he had packed. The cats were lying in a large pool of sunlight on the kitchen counter, washing themselves. Simon realized that he was hungry and looked in the refrigerator. He found a half-empty pint of milk, a stick of margarine with toast crumbs embedded in one of its ends, a half pound of bacon ends and scraps, a can of sauerkraut juice, a bowl with two desiccated-looking chicken wings in it, a jar of rock-solid grated cheese, a frozen-orange-juice can with bacon grease in it, two wrinkled green apples, three eggs, mayonnaise, two flashlight batteries, a bunch of brown carrots with wilted tops, mustard, horseradish, relish, a slice of onion wrapped in aluminum foil, a wine bottle with less than an inch of wine in it, three slices of protein bread in a plastic bag, and a wedge of moldy Cheddar cheese. He wondered idly whether he would someday have children of his own, and whether after they had left home the contents of his refrigerator would be like this, and these speculations made him realize that his life and life in general would continue no matter what happened to his brother. He decided he could have something to eat when he got to the city.

III

Nick went into a coma for four days. He did not wake or move—except to be turned to avoid bedsores—or, as far as anyone knew, dream or think, or in any other clear way seem to traffic with the numberless fine and gross alterations that create time. Because Nick was between life and death, between time and no-time, more nearly an object in time than a subject of it, and because he was the sole focus of Simon's life, the four days were, for Simon, less like days than space or volume, a physical structure inhabited as a house is inhabited, the days like suites, the hours like rooms, the minutes like the air in those rooms. He would take a turn at sleeping in the apartment across from the hospital and waken not knowing whether it was day or night. He ate breakfast at seven-thirty at night and lunch after midnight. In the morning or evening, he would look out a window at the street in front of the hospital and be momentarily baffled by the surge of cars he saw there, and then he would think, Oh, yes—it must be rush hour. Newspapers mystified him, as if they were dispatches from some other universe.

He was in a dance, a sort of minuet with his mother and father and Louise and Nancy, with Nicky at the still center of the circle. He went out for a walk with his mother one cold, clear afternoon. Emily said, "You know, I just had a small argument with Nancy. They want only one of us sitting with Nicky at a time, and Nancy and I were both planning to go in, and she actually said, 'I have more right than you do.' I wanted to say, 'But he's my son.' " Simon said, "She's just upset." Later that day, he was sitting in the lounge with his father. Joe said, "I'm worried about your mother. We had breakfast in the cafeteria this morning, and she had almost no appetite at all. Even in the worst emergency, that woman will eat a healthy meal." Simon said, "She'll be all right. Everybody sleeps—I mean eats too much anyway." He had to reassure Louise that she belonged with the family, that she wasn't in the way, and he listened while Nancy told him that Nick could hardly stand the pressure and competitiveness at his law firm, and envied Simon the more relaxed life of a teacher. Simon knew that he was being talked about, too—that the others, in various pairs and combinations, and always with Nick at the heart of their concern, were weaving him into the web of words with which they were all trying to catch and hold him.

It was agreed that if Nick took any sort of turn, for the better or for the worse, whoever was in the hospital at the time would call the apartment across the street or go over to it, to tell whoever was resting there what had happened. Simon and Louise were sleeping there one afternoon when the door-bell rang. Simon, who had been sleeping in his clothes, rushed to the door and opened it. A stranger stood there—a very short, dark-haired woman holding what looked like an oversized briefcase. "Avon calling," she said. Simon said, "We don't want anything, but I can't tell you how happy I am that it's you."

Not long after that, Nick's kidneys shut down completely. In the lounge, the tall resident explained to the family, in his formal way, how dangerous this turn of events was, and said that he and the surgeon and a consulting doctor on the case thought that they should start Nick on peritoneal dialysis, to remove the poisons that had begun to accumulate in his blood.

By late that night, the dialysis had cleared Nick's blood enough to bring him near consciousness. Simon stood in the doorway of the room with his father and Louise and watched while Emily and Nancy loudly called Nick's name and implored him to wake up. Nick moved his head back and forth, and then opened his eyes for a second and smiled faintly, almost mischievously, as if he knew some wonderful secret he wanted to tease them with but not tell them. He closed his eyes again, and the resident, who was also in the room, stepped forward—eagerly, like an ungainly girl who has wanted to dance all night and has finally been asked —checked Nick's pulse and pupils, and said that he was in something more nearly like real sleep than a coma. He shooed everyone except the private nurse out, and they all tiptoed away, smiling. Simon took Louise's hand. She began to cry, and they stopped so that the others would go ahead. "I'm sorry," she said. "It's just such a relief."

The resident came up behind Simon and drew him away. "I wanted to say that although we have an improvement, it may be a temporary result of the dialysis. It's not clear that this is the beginning of a recovery."

"But you're more hopeful?" Simon said.

"Well, yes, but it's not entirely, um, rational. Anything can happen."

"O.K., thank you," Simon said. "Listen, I also want to thank you for your help in all of this. I don't know what your regular duties are, what your assignment is, but I do know that you've spent more than the normal amount of time and effort with my brother."

"It's an unusual case," the resident said.

"It's not just that. That's the kind of thing that I would say, but I know it's more than that, and I'm grateful for your concern."

In the lounge, everyone chatted cheerfully for a while.

Then Nancy and Emily said they wanted to try to get some sleep. "If you're not too exhausted to stay here, my lamb," Emily said to Simon.

"No, I feel fine," Simon said. "You go on. Joe, you go too."

Simon and Louise slept on the couches for a few hours. Just before dawn, Simon dreamed that he was his brother, and that someone was trying to rouse him from a deep sleep. He awoke to find Nick's private-duty nurse gently shaking his shoulder. He said, "Where's Simon?"

"You're Simon, aren't you?" the nurse said.

"Yes. I'm sorry. I guess I was dreaming."

"Well, excuse me for disturbing you, but your brother's awake and he asked to see you."

"Is he all right?" Simon asked as he stood up from the couch. Louise was awake, too.

"He seems to be quite alert," the nurse said.

"I'll call my parents," Simon said.

"But he asked to see you."

"You go on, Si," Louise said sleepily. "He just wants to see you."

Simon followed the nurse to Nick's room. She let him go in alone. He walked in and stood at the foot of the bed. Nick's head and shoulders were propped up on some pillows.

"I think that was almost the ballgame," Nick said weakly. "How long was I out?"

"A few days. It wasn't the ballgame, though, so don't worry."

"Where are Joe and Em?"

"Over at the apartment with Nancy. They're sleeping."

"Our apartment?"

"Oh, no, that's right, you couldn't have known, what with all your malingering," Simon said. "There's a nurses' and residents' residence"—he gestured with one hand, to acknowledge the repetition—"and we've all been taking care—taking turns sleeping there."

"Why don't you sit down, my young scholar? You look like a tombstone standing there."

Simon went around the bed and sat in the chair next to the head. He leaned forward, put his hands between his knees, curved his shoulders in and held his arms tight against his sides, like a child learning to dive.

"What do the doctors say?"

"Your kidneys weren't working too well, and that's one reason you were unconscious for so long. Urea or uric acid. I forget which it is. Maybe both. They built up in your blood, so they put you on this abdominal dialysis, and that cleared your blood up and you woke up. You're going to be fine now. You really had us scared."

"I'm still incredibly tired, but for some reason I'm not so scared myself now. Is the infection better?"

"You wouldn't be awake if it weren't better," Simon said.

"How's Nancy?" Nick asked.

"Fine. We're all O.K."

"Christ, my arm aches," Nick said.

"It's from the tubes."

"Suddenly I feel just terrible again."

"Well, you don't look bad at all, considering. The nurse shaved you yesterday, and your color isn't bad."

"You're supposed to be sick," Nick said.

"I'm all better. A nurse gave me a shot of penicillin. She was very cute."

"But are you cold?" Nick said. "You look all hunched up."

"No, I'm fine," Simon said. He took his hands from between his knees and sat back in the chair. He managed to relax a little, but only by an effort of will.

"I feel like I can't really get my breath," Nick said.

"Do you want the nurse?"

"What's she going to do—breathe for me?"

"I'm sorry. I thought she might be able to help. Or the doctor."

"Sorry, Si. It's just that I feel so crummy."

"Forget it."

Nicholas closed his eyes. Simon sat forward, and then began to get up from the chair. Nicholas waved his right hand feebly. "I'm O.K.," he said. "Just resting. Stick around."

Simon sat down. The room was quiet. He looked at his brother. He thought, If I had to and if there were some way of doing it, I would give my life for his. At first, although he had not the slightest doubt that it was true, the thought astonished him. It seemed like an arrow that had been shot into him from a distance so great that the archer could not be seen or a silent predator that had tracked him down and at last cornered him here in this bare, still place. But then he realized that it had been in him somewhere from the very moment his mother had called him at school—nothing inimical or alien but part of himself.

The room was filled with a kind of pewter light. Nothing moved. It was as though the pendulum of every clock in the world had stopped for a moment at the top of its arc. Nick opened his eyes and smiled. "Is Joe all right?" he asked, but his eyes seemed to be asking some other question. He turned his head toward the door and said, with a tone of genuine curiosity, "Who's that?"

"There's no one there, Nicky."

Nicholas turned his face back toward Simon. He said, firmly, "Si, this is it." He took a deep breath, like someone who is about to dive down to the bottom of a lake to find something valuable he has lost there, and then he died.

Simon became aware of the hissing of the heating vent behind him. He turned and saw that the curtain hanging over it was moving slightly. He stood up and closed his brother's eyes, and then he sat down again and cried.

IV

Nancy went to the apartment on Henry Street by taxi. She would get her car and drive up to Palisades later in the day. Louise and Simon sat in the back seat of Joe's car. Joe drove and Emily sat in front. As they made their way out of the parking lot, the sun, just above the horizon, caught a window in the hospital and set it ablaze. Joe stopped the car before pulling out onto the avenue. He said, "Simon, which—"

"You go left here, Joe," Simon said.

ALICE ADAMS

Time in Santa Fe

IT IS MID-AFTERNOON, on a brilliant August day, and I am sitting in a darkened bar, here in Santa Fe. I am drinking white wine with Jeffrey, an old friend who at any moment is going to tell me about his new gay life. I do not especially look forward to hearing his story; nothing against gayness, it is just that I have problems of my own that seem to make me selfish, a poor listener—although, being very fond of Jeffrey, I plan to make an effort.

We have a window table, and at this odd hour there is no one in the bar but us and the lanky, bored bartender, who is almost invisible, behind the bar, in the shadowy depths of the room. We can look out across Sante Fe's central square, the Plaza, where some Indians ('native craftsmen') have set up tables of brass jewelry, dazzling, flashing white-gold, in the violently pure sunlight. On the other side of the Plaza more native craftspersons sit or squat behind their wares, over there mostly silver and turquoise. They are sheltered by the wide, outspread tiled eaves of an ancient Spanish building. And, spreading over everything is the extraordinary, vast Southwestern sky, its white clouds massed into sculptured monuments, incredibly slow-moving, and immense.

Neither Jeffrey nor I is much of a drinker, really; this bar simply seemed the only plausible thing for us to do next. In the morning, after my plane came in to Albuquerque, where

Jeff met me and drove me up here, we walked up the
Canyon Road; we 'did' a lot of galleries there, and shops.
We saw nearly the same paintings, same jewelry and rugs
and embroidered clothing over and over again, repeated
everywhere, until we both felt choked with the sight of so
much merchandise (we are neither of us buyers, or shop-
pers, really; even rich, or richer, we probably would not
be). We had an early lunch in a place where you have to
stand in line, but that was nice, standing in the warm noon
sunshine, in a patio of flowers; and for lunch we had something made with blue tortillas—I could hardly believe it, a
rich dark blue, blue flour, Jeff said, and delicious.

Then we walked around the Plaza for a while, looking
into more stores, but the pause for lunch had not renewed
our interest in things for sale, and the day had begun to
seem very, very hot. And so, when Jeffrey said, "Well, how
about a nice cold glass of wine?" I said, "Great, great idea."
We both knew that sooner or later we would have to talk
about things, to say how we both were, and maybe some
wine would help.

Jeffrey has had the same thick soft brown beard for the
fifteen years that we have known each other (we first met in
Berkeley, as students; I was just married then, and very
pregnant) but when we were outside, in the merciless bright
unimpeded sunlight, I could see some gray threads in the
dark of his beard, and a few in his hair, which he still wears
almost as long as he did in those old days. At that time
Jeffrey was having a relationship (we all assumed) with a
friend of his, David; but then, a few years later, he married
Susan, a lawyer, blond and goodlooking (sort of). Now,
having split from Susan, the new assumption is that he is
gay again (David lives here too) and that he comes to Santa
Fe to be gay, as well as to paint. So far, we have only talked
very casually about mutual friends; I notice that we have
not discussed either Susan or my husband, Rick. And, come
to think of it, we have barely mentioned David; Jeffrey has

only said that he is not here, he is visiting his mother in La Jolla.

I have just been visiting my own mother in Austin, Texas; this side trip to see Jeffrey before going home to Petaluma is an indulgence, but not much of one: juggling new airfares, going home an odd route through Denver, it only costs twenty dollars more than not stopping at all would have. Anyway, my mother has become an alcoholic, and a recluse, almost. She sits there all day, sipping sherry and smoking and watching soaps on TV, like someone a great deal older than she actually is. And she looks much older, too; she is both puffy and withered, at barely sixty. I don't know what to do about her.

Another problem on my mind is Rick. He is a building contractor; that seemed an eminently sensible move, from skilled carpenter to contractor, ten years ago, in the financially optimistic early seventies. But now he is out of work, and he is enraged—at everything in the world, me included. I have a teaching job, fourth grade, and so we are not as badly off as many people, but Rick keeps saying that I could be laid off too, which is true, of course, but I think in a way he hates it that I am the one still working, and it makes him hate me, a lot of the time.

And, more worries: Barbara, our daughter, who is only fifteen, wants to marry her boyfriend, Brad, who is all of eighteen (it is very possible that she either is or thinks she is pregnant).

And (this is sad): our old cat, Puss, who is almost fifteen, a sort of wedding present, has almost stopped eating.

For some reason Puss is the one I think about the most, I don't know why. It is true that I love her very much; she is such an outrageous calico, with a bright orange patch on one eye, and a yellow stomach. We have been through a lot together, as it were. But I love those people too, my mother and Rick and Barbara, all of them, very much. Maybe in a way it is easier to think about Puss? And of course she is the only one who does not talk back; when, in my mind, I tell my mother to drink less, and tell Barbara not to get married and Rick not to be so angry, they all have a lot to say to me, in return (and this goes on all day, like a radio that I can't turn off).

I suddenly remember that Jeffrey has always had cats, and so I ask him, "Do you have a cat now, down here?"

He smiles, one faithful cat lover to another, and he says, "Of course. Actually we have three, a mother and two sons. The kittens were so cute we couldn't give them up. You know how that goes."

The 'we' must mean David, whom of course I should ask about, but I am not quite ready for that. Easier to go on about cats. I tell him that I am a little worried about Puss, her not eating.

And Jeffrey remembers Puss—how endearing of him! "A really great cat," he proclaims, as I beam. And he goes on, "Who could forget an orange eye patch like that?" He tells me not to worry too much about her non-eating. Sometimes an older cat will just be off her feed for a while, he says, the way people sometimes are. He also says that he has a friend here in town with a beautiful calico cat who is *twenty-one years old*.

This is the best news I've heard in months, a cat that old. It is so good it makes me laugh. "Wow, twenty-one. I'll tell Puss she has to make it that far."

Jeffrey laughs too. "Well, sure she will."

However, my plane to Denver is not until ten tonight, and we can't talk about cats all that time, although in a way I would like to.

And so, in a plunging-in way I ask him, "Well, how's David?"

Deliberately Jeffrey takes a drink of his wine, before he says, "Well, actually not too good. He had an operation, one of those real uglies. You know, they say they got every-thing? But you're so damaged. David is so damaged, I mean. That's what this trip to see his mother is all about. We don't know what to expect, really. Or when."

"Oh, Jeffrey." I reach across the table and take his hands, remembering as I do so, as I touch them, what beautiful long hands Jeffrey has. Holding hands for a moment we just look at each other—nothing else to do. I say, "I'm really sorry."

"Well, you're nice, but don't be sorry. We'll manage. And right now he's really okay. We're just sort of playing it by ear, day to day." As we both retrieve our hands, he adds, "He'll be sorry he didn't see you, of course. He sends love."

"Oh! Please give him my love."

We sit there quietly for several minutes, then, adjusting to the presence of this awful news of David, lying there between us like a stone.

Often, lately, as I castigate myself for such self-absorption in my own forms of trouble, I have thought about people in refugee camps, in the Middle East, or starving people anywhere, the hopeless, the genuinely anguished population of the world. But here is Jeffrey, directly in front of me, and while his troubles are nowhere near the horrible pains of those people, still his are considerably worse than mine, I think: a possibly (probably) dying loved person.

Like many shy people, Jeffrey tends to come out of silences into small speeches, that have the sound of paragraphs. He always has (fifteen years is always); he does so now. "One thing I've meant to say to you," he says, in our silence, in the sun-moted room, "is that, uh, splitting with Susan had nothing to do with David. Although it could have looked like that. But she took off with a guy from art school. I felt pretty bad, and David said why not come down here. He was living with somebody at the time, and so the three of us shared a house for a while, which I have to say was not all that great." He gives me a twisting smile.

"I'll bet not," I tell him, trying to imagine how that would be: me and Rick and—and who?

"Anyway, then the other guy left, and there we were again, roommates. And then David got sick."

"*God,* Jeffrey."

"Yeah."

At that moment everything in our minds—in mine, for sure, and surely in Jeff's too—is so awful that as we look at each other across the table we begin to laugh, like nuts, or drunks (the bartender must think we've been drinking all day). We laugh and laugh, and when one of us stops the other starts off again. We exhaust ourselves.

"Oh God," he says, finally, wiping at his eyes with a big clean handkerchief. "Oh God, I'm so glad you came here to see me."

"Wait until I tell you all about my life," I say to him. "That'll really cheer you up." Which sets us off again, into minor hysterics.

Finally, we sober up, so that I can tell him in an abbreviated way about my people, my concerns over them. He has never met my mother, and he only knew Barbara as a small child, and so it is Rick that I mostly talk about. "Basically he's just very depressed," I say. "And instead of cheering him up I get depressed too, and that makes him feel worse. It's just so difficult, people living together, isn't it."

Jeffrey speaks slowly, and very thoughtfully. "Sometimes it does help, though," he says, "if you just accept the fact that you can't do a lot for anyone else. Then you stop trying so hard, and worrying over what feels like failure."

I consider this; it seems sensible, and even helpful. It is true that I can't do a lot for Rick, beyond being there, which sometimes he doesn't want. (Will he be more glad to see me after this trip? I have wondered.)

Jeffrey looks at his watch, just then, and I do too. It is much later than either of us imagined. We have talked for a long time. "I thought we'd have dinner here in town," Jeff says, "but now I wonder: maybe you'd rather come out to the house, and I'll rustle up a snack?"

"Oh, I'd really like that."

"I'd like you to see it." He smiles, adding, "And the cats."
More soberly, a little anxiously, he further adds, "I really
mean snack, though. With David gone I haven't been eating
a lot. Like your Puss, I'm off my feed." Another smile.

"Well, I'd love to see your house. And the cats. And a
snack would be great."

Once we have made this plan it seems so obviously what
we should do that I wonder why Jeffrey didn't suggest it before; of course I would want to see his house and cats. And a
tiny question flashes into my mind: could Jeffrey possibly
have had some worry or shyness at the idea of our being
alone, in an empty house, with David away at his mother's
and Rick up in Petaluma? Just possibly he had, although
there had never been a suggestion of that sort of feeling
between us. Gayness aside, we are not each other's sexual
types. Both being dark (we look just slightly alike, come to
think of it: tall dark shy people who smile a lot), we both
seem drawn to blond people. Rick is the blondest of all, big
white-blond Swedish Rick, and David is blond, and so
was—is—Susan. But you can't tell; sometimes men just
think they are supposed to come on to you, at the oddest
times. The oddest men.

We get out of the bar and we tread across the Plaza, past
all the blindingly bright brass, and the Indians, to Jeffrey's
car. His house is out on something called Bishop's Lodge
Road, he tells me, maybe fifteen minutes out of town.

And, generous Jeff, he seems to have been thinking about
my problems. (He has always been like that, I remember.
Maybe that is a reason I came to see him?) Specifically, he
has thought about my mother. "If she really doesn't care
about her life, or looking good," he says, "if she just wants
to anesthetize herself, I think you have to let her. What else
can you do? Maybe this is the happiest she could be. I think
you worry too much."

I can see that he is right, probably, and I am grateful—but

at the moment it is hard for me to focus on my mother, in Austin; I am so overwhelmed by everything I see, the sand and rocks and sagebrush, the sheer stretch of space. Every shape, each color seems entirely new to me, and it is all so much larger and grander than anything, anywhere, that I ever saw before.

Jeffrey's house is small, a white adobe shack, on a dirt road up off the highway—on a hill, with astounding views of further rocky, sandy hills, strange gray-green desert vegetation. We park and go into the house, and at first I think there is only one room, with a kitchen and long trestle table at one end. Some low couches, pillows, Indian rugs. But then I make out a sleeping loft. Still, hardly room for three people, David and his former lover, and Jeff—poor Jeff.

"Well, another glass of wine? We might as well?" Jeffrey begins to rummage about in the kitchen, and I see that I was right; having me here is making him nervous.

"Oh, it's so beautiful here," I tell him. "I really wish Rick could see it. And Barbara, actually, the dumb kid."

Happily, he seizes on this. "Well, why not?" in an eager way he asks me. "You could all come down? Even when David's back, we'd make do. You know, pretend it's fifteen years ago, and we're all sleeping around in bags."

We both laugh, and somehow the very idea of those absent people, my people, and his, has made Jeffrey easy with me again, and that silly bad moment is over.

The cats are something of a disappointment, though; scrawny and shy, they lack style, or maybe I've been spoiled by glamorous Puss. But I pat them and scratch their ears, and I tell Jeffrey that they are nice. What is actually nice is touching a cat at all. My mother is allergic to them, and so I had not had my hands on a cat for a week; it was like getting a fix.

All around us, on the walls, are big canvasses, filled with huge dim gray-green shapes, like mirrors on the desert. No way to tell whether the paintings are Jeffrey's or David's, and it doesn't seem right to ask. In any case, they are so much a part of the room, as well as the landscape, that it feels unnecessary to remark on them at all.

For supper Jeffrey makes us omelettes with sour cream and some greenish Mexican glop that I don't much like, but I appreciate his effort, of course. Most of all I appreciate the fact that my spirits have lightened, quite a lot; I really feel okay.

He makes very good coffee. It has the faintest taste of chocolate, and we talk some more, drinking coffee.

I'm really worried over Rick, and my mother, and Barbara. And Puss. That is what, in effect, I say.

And Jeffrey says that he is worried and sad about David.

And we say to each other that we must not worry.

We are like people holding hands through a disaster, I think.

Later still, Jeffrey drives me down across the now-darkened desert to Albuquerque, to my plane, and on the way he tells me that he was serious about our visiting, all of us. "Or any one or two of you," he says, with a little laugh.

I tell him that it is a nice idea, nice of him, but in a practical way it seems very unlikely indeed, and I urge him to come up to see us, in Northern California.

However, as I settle into my seat on the plane, and buckle in, headed for Denver (which is certainly a long way to go, to get to Petaluma, California), then, along with a return of worry about what I am headed for, my same old problems, and my flying fears, I also experience a shot of warmth, of true comfort: there is Jeffrey, more or less permanently, in a place that I now have seen, and can visualize. Where I would always be welcome.

I smile to myself, in the dark, as I loftily imagine that I am speeding through fields of stars. I feel suddenly rich.

The Battle of Boiling Water

WE HAD A DEPRESSION PLANT right in the middle of
our dining room table: a piece of Pennsylvania coal, planted
as though it were a living thing, in a strange ground made
up of chemicals and dyes, specially chosen and carefully
arranged upon a platter of cut glass. The Depression Plant
seemed to be growing; it was shaped like a mountain, and I
used to spend hours watching sick little forests of purple
and green and white crystals climb its small, alpine valleys,
and gradually conceal the mass of black on which they
grew.

Outside, The Bonus Army was getting ready to march on
Washington. I knew all about it. All through the dark Pittsburgh winter, unemployed men had been coming to our
kitchen door asking for coffee or cigarettes or shoes, and I
would stare out at them from behind my mother, and sometimes talk to them. I saw where they lived, too, when we
went to Old Saint Patrick's Church, once a month, for
the Lourdes Novena. The church was right next to the
railroad, near the freight yards of the Union Depot, and
that was where the men lived, in Shantytown. Going past
Shantytown was the most exciting part of the trip to the
Lourdes Novena. My father tried to march us past it briskly
in a military formation, but I would always hang back, for I
wanted to see it. I would ask questions; but he would only
say, angrily, that something was rotten with America, or

that Andy Mellon should be taken out and shot; then he would hurry me on, to the Novena.

I liked the inside of Old Saint Patrick's Church, for it was not really a church at all. Half of it, all down one side, was given over to a full-sized model or replica of the Grotto in Lourdes, France, where Our Lady of the Immaculate Conception had appeared nine times in a row to a shepherd girl named Bernadette Soubirous. I was captivated and filled with delight that anyone would think of bringing a thing like that in from outside, and putting it in a church; that was better than the shanties, even.

The man who had done it was Father Cox. He was not as good as Father Coughlin, but almost. He had brought stones from the very spot in France where Our Lady had stood, and the men from Shantytown had come, being out of work, and had built the huge shrine for him. It had everything, candles, and Vigil lights, and even sheep. There was ivy, all up and down the rocks of the grotto; then there was Bernadette, kneeling, beside a real spring of real water; and finally, there was our Blessed Lady, high up above everything, with roses on her feet. There were crutches, and canes, and medical braces, as well, left there by people who had been cured by the Lourdes Water, and some of the crutches, I knew, were from the men wounded in the war.

The service ended with the singing of the Lourdes Hymn, "Ave, Ave, Ave Maria," which I could sing very well, and which I sang very loudly, for I wanted to be like Father Cox, and Father Coughlin; I wanted to grow up, and be a priest, and help lead the men.

But to tell the truth, I was not happy as I sang. I had done something wrong, you see. I had committed a sin. That was not too bad, perhaps; I knew from catechism class that every human being was guilty of some sin, and needed to be forgiven. But that was the whole point. My particular failure had been so private, and so personal, and so embarrassing that I could not bring myself to talk about it, even in the Confessional. I went up to Confession one Saturday afternoon, at my home church, and waited in line; and when the time came I told all my faults but the one humiliating thing. When the priest asked, "Is that all, Son?" I lied; I said "Yes." And when it was over I had held back a sin in Confession, something I had heard that other people did, but something I had never, never in my life, thought that I would be capable of.

And the following week it wasn't any easier, for now I really had something difficult to mention; at first I only had the thing that I had done by myself in the bedroom, but now I had held back a sin in Confession; I had received a Sacrament unworthily. I had committed therefore what the Catechism called a Sacrilege: I had lied to God. And how could I ever manage to tell that to anybody?

How had I gotten myself into such a state? It is a long, painful story.

There was a very attractive girl at school named Jean Marie Mangan. She was the brightest girl in class, and I was the brightest boy. I remember telling my sister once, in a flush of honesty, that there was a girl just like her at school. I liked Jean Marie Mangan—no, I loved her—but she was the enemy; she competed with me for every prize. We spent years "trapping" one another in recitation line; she would go up, in Mathematics, and I would go down; but then I would go up in Geography, and she would go down; and we both pointedly ignored one another, on the way up, and on the way down.

All the same, I loved her, and carried everywhere within me her double: a Jean Marie Mangan faithful in every detail of walk, and word, and gesture, but one much more approachable, who let herself be talked to. And I talked to her, in a far more kind and gentlemanly way than I ever did to the real one.

In public, however, our rivalry was intense. We pointedly ignored one another on the way to school, too; even when we happened to drop into Isaly's Dairy Store together, only disparaging comments were exchanged.

Not everyone was fooled, however. A pimply-faced young man behind the ice cream counter there saw every-thing. He knew; oh, he *knew,* all right; he knew everything. He was a Protestant, and much older than I. He teased me about being a Roman Catholic; it was from his lips I first heard of "The Battle of Boiling Water." He meant the famous Battle of the River Boyne, in Ireland, of course, where King James the Second was defeated by William of Orange, but neither of us knew that:

> "Ten thousand Micks—
> —"Lost their necks—" he would sing to me
>   as he worked
> "—At the *Battle of Boiling Water!*"

It was a warfare we carried on. I could not get away from him; whenever he saw me coming he was always free. I would order my ice-cream cone, and wait, with my nickel on the counter, but it took him forever. And after he got done singing The Battle of Boiling Water, he eventually got around to the subject of girls.

Today, I realize that with that Emperor of Ice Cream, it was a labor of love; that he spent most of the day sculpting and moulding enormous, pointed, uproariously phallic cones for the parochial school children of Pittsburgh. He was a teacher; he educated, while he worked; a stream of under-breath mutterings of every kind of obscenity ex-plained all man needed to know. And the last words he always said to me as he handed me my over-sized, pinnacled cone, the words I could always clearly hear, were, "Ooooooh—He *played* with it!"

I hated his talk, but I loved ice-cream, and as long as I had the money to spend, we fought each time, the Battle of the Boyne. Which I now know I lost.

One Thursday, after the Protestant forces had vanquished for the thousandth time the last of the Catholic Stuarts in that miserable, hateful old battle, I found myself singing again, in the weekly choir practice. Jean Mangan and I competed at this, too. We stood directly across the aisle from one another, singing very hard. That day we were practicing a hymn called *"Peace, It is I!"*, a song such as a boy would like, for it was full of shipwrecks, tempests, billows, and a strange, impossible monster called "The Whale of Euroclydon." "Whale of Euroclydon," we sang, "Be thou at rest!", not knowing what it was we were singing about. I sang it better than anyone, for I was the only one who could really pronounce the word. I was the one who got us past "Euroclydon," and I was very proud. But as I sang that day before the Lord my God the hymn *"Peace, It is I!"* and appeared to gaze most intently at the Tabernacle upon the altar, I knew very well that my eyes were really only upon the lovely face and body of Jean Marie Mangan, and I was hoping that she heard.

Something had to be done. I recalled the things that had been said to me. The young man at Isaly's had congratulated me openly upon her again and again; he had suggested that riotous things must have already taken place, or if they had not, were vastly overdue. He was a fool, of course, and yet I knew that a fight was building up; that sooner or later that fight must be fought; and that if I did not win it, I would never be a priest.

What ridicule would I have endured had he really known the truth? For the truth was that for many weeks now, months even, I had longed to run away and leave Pittsburgh forever, in the company of Jean Marie Mangan, and did so, in my imagination, many times a day. On each trip to the grocery I escaped with her to those strange places that I knew so much about: to the banks of the Indus and the Oxus; the rock-carved city of Petra, in the desert; then far, far beyond, to the Upper Kingdom of old Egypt, past the Six Great Cataracts, even to the Sources of the Nile. But always, always, most of all, last of all, to fabled Samarkand. We rode on Bactrian camels, which I knew from Geography were the ones with two humps, and I defended her from all dangers, including, even, sometimes, in some rather unusual circumstances, the Whale of Euroclydon.

And yet who was really the fool; for I loved the world, and I loved Jean Mangan; but I knew that I could never really go to Samarkand with her, or any place, if I was to become a priest.

Something did have to be done therefore; and I wondered, as I sang, what I was to do.

When I got home, I still had not thought of a solution, so I went down into the cellar, for I wanted to think, and that was where I thought.

There were books down there — discarded, extra books, too large or too worn to be kept in the living room upstairs. There were books on fishing, and mountain climbing, and gardening, in among old *National Geographic* magazines. My sea books were there, too, with splendid color pictures of *H.M.S. Repulse* and *H.M.S. Renown* firing broadsides off Gibraltar, and of SS Orantes passing the Seven Sisters. But the book I liked most of all, and the one that always set me thinking best, was *The Wonder Book of the World*. It was large, and beautifully bound, with leather that had come from Morocco, my Father said; its cover had a Nautical Compass embossed upon it, in the center, with a boy riding a dolphin through the waves, out toward each of its corners. I often wondered how the boy stayed on, and what it must be like to glide from wave to wave, and to plunge into the green depths, and whether he could breathe or not under water. Once when I was swimming at North Park I tried it; dunked my head under the water and opened my eyes. Everything was green and blue, and all sounds became squeals as I felt the pressure of depth. I tried swallowing, without opening my mouth; but the strange, orgasmic squeak that I heard surprised me, and I surfaced at once. All the same, I loved the big book, and was fond of turning its pages, thinking of what I would be when I grew up.

Before I had even gotten to the Great Pyramid of Cheops that day, I knew what I should do.

I went up to my bedroom, and took down *H.M.S. Agamemnon,* pride of the Royal Navy, from my dresser, and put it on the mantle. Then I found a statue of Our Blessed Lady, and a box of Mother's Oats, which was round and strong and could serve as a hidden base. I emptied the cereal into a bowl, and stood the statue of Our Lady upon the box, and surrounded it with a cloth, spraying it with paint; and soon I had my own grotto, complete with tiny crutches, even, made from match sticks. I placed a bottle of Lourdes Water beside it all, from Old Saint Patrick's Church, and as I lit the Vigil light in front of it, made a vow to Our Blessed Lady that I would become a priest, and would help to save the world.

For a whole week I did not think of Jean Mangan—or at least did not go on any imaginary voyages with her, though it was hard keeping her out of trips to the Karakorums, or to the Steppes of Central Asia. All through the week I read with growing excitement what Father Cox had to say about the Soldier's Bonus and the impending march on Washington. I even returned the taunts of the young man at Isaly's, secure in the knowledge of my secret grotto (whence all my strength came). I played ball on Dunlap Street with coarse companions, and at certain very strategic moments of the day, went home to light the Vigil light to renew my consecration. And yet, by the end of the week I had fallen, in the manner I have described.

After that, life became very difficult. I was, essentially, waiting to go to Confession. The thing to do was to confess my failure as quickly as possible, and to start over.

But when Saturday came, and I found that, because of one, pitiful small detail in the matter, I could not bring myself to confess it, everything became awful.

The days were all right. For one thing, I was good at baseball as it was played in the streets. I was generally chosen first, to bat third, and to be "clean-up" man. I would stand at the man-hole cover we used for Home-plate, and hit the ball over the head of the last little child who was "backing up" away down the block, and who was supposed to keep the ball from rolling into Ritchey Street sewer; and while he chased it I would stride triumphantly around the bases, to the admiration of my companions, all but forgetting that I had held back a sin in Confession.

But the nights were different. For then I had to go home, and face my problem with God, alone; and my God was a fierce God.

I had the soundest theological authority for believing that because I had committed what was called a Mortal Sin, and then had gone on to commit yet another, more serious sin of Sacrilege, I had left Him no choice. He would rightly — indeed, could in no way do otherwise, and truly be God — cast me into eternal damnation. And it was not just a case of what the Catechism said, either, or certain great theologians; the New Testament itself was uncompromising on such things: "Depart from me, Ye cursed," it said, "into everlasting fire," and talked of the "exterior darkness," where there was weeping, and gnashing of teeth. It said it over and over in different ways. It spoke of an unquenchable fire, and an unquenchable thirst; and it seemed to me that whenever I went to the Bible for help, it always fell open at such places.

And yet, I did not want to be judged on any weaker grounds.

Only when morning came, and the sun shone, and the light of day made things seem not quite so bad, I reneged, and went to school, and played ball, and so guaranteed that I would face my problems once more in the same old way, on a bed of pain, and in the darkness of the night.

I began not to be able to put up with it, falling into fitful periods of sleep that was not sleep, half dreaming, half worrying; I seemed far out at sea, like that boy on a dolphin, the last lonely clanging bell that marked anything having been left far behind; and it was in this melancholy seascape of long, deep ocean swells, of parting and of closing mists, of muffled distances and of the cries of unknown sea-birds, that I first spied or sensed or felt that strange creature from the Antipodes: the whale, my own special whale, Euroclydon, that has never left me. "Whale of Euroclydon, Be thou at rest," I said, weakly, hopelessly. Oh, I did not see him, I knew that; I more heard him, or felt him, along the region of the heart; but I knew what he was like. I felt that his arrival was long overdue; I felt, even, relieved, that it was about time we should be introduced.

As the night wore on, I could not fall asleep, often, for I was beginning to be conscious of what would happen if I should die during the night. Here was a whole new horror, which had not occurred to me before. I began to not want to fall sleep.

I listened to my heart. It was beating faithfully; indeed it seemed the one faithful thing I had in the circumstances, and so I talked to it in the darkness; I became wonderfully aware of how all life was really only one heart-beat away from nothing. And so I urged my heart on; and I remember promising it that if it would do its share, and get us both safely into the morning, I would do the rest; I would get up and go to Confession and clear the whole thing up, so that I and my body and my conscience and my heart could all live merrily together and at peace once again.

I tried to pray. I lit the Vigil light in front of Our Lady's statue, but the flickering wick only cast more shadows into the room, and the pathetic little grotto only reminded me of all my previous foolishnesses, my vain hopes, and wild ambitions, and so I put the flame out. And in the dark that followed, I tried singing: "Whale of Euroclydon," I sang, "Be thou at rest!" but softly, so that he might hear, and no one else.

I began to argue. Finally I could take it no more. I realized perfectly well that a person in the state of sin had no right to pray to God, that the only prayers of his that had a chance of being answered were those which asked for a release from that state, and these I could not or would not utter. I began to feel, vaguely, put upon, for I knew that boys were not supposed to undergo such things; my friends in the street obviously did not. And so I began to argue with Him; what kind of God was it that let a person get into something like this? What kind of God did He think He was anyway? And what about crippled children? If he was so good, how did it happen that everything was so all screwed up? Why did everything need saving, anyway?

Then I would become frightened, and think about what I had said; I had presumed to question my Maker: I would be damned now more than before, if that was possible. I turned over fiercely in my bed, and listened to the old house creak; no one else, apparently, was having any trouble. And I went to sleep, only to dream: of that creature nine fathoms deep, underneath the keel, from the land of mist and snow. It was Euroclydon; for make no mistake, he was out there somewhere, only he was waiting; he had all the time in the world. A special whale, for those who had lied to God. And I would wake up, seeing that baleful eye, and almost shouting. But no: the Grotto was still there, and *H.M.S. Agamemnon* as well, outlined by the light from the street-lamp. And so I popped, a ridiculous young boy, from Jonah to Job, and from Job back to Jonah again; and I still don't understand what business I had with any of it.

And so, night after night, I wrestled with God — or rather with the idea of Him, for I was beginning to think He no longer existed. My fight was now no longer with flesh and blood; it was no longer about Jean Mangan, even. I began to doubt: no god could be that cruel. The books in Carnegie Library were true, then, that said there wasn't any, and that my Faith was wrong. And that made the fellow at Isaly's probably right, about the Battle of Boiling Water.... At last, I hoped that my God would go away, and take his church, and his whale, and his priesthood with him.

I cannot say that God came to me in the whirlwind, or that he spoke to me, or that he even helped me at all. But one Friday evening in May, after a satisfactory afternoon of hitting the ball very far down Ruggles Street again and again, I came home determined to do something about my problem. I ate supper, and read the papers, to see what was going on with the world and with the men; then I went down in the cellar to think. I went over to the books and glanced through one about the Knights of the Round Table, and another on Schlieman's discovery of the site of ancient Troy. I spent the rest of the hour paging through one of my mountain-climbing books, about the Himalayas.

But I was procrastinating, for the book I wanted was called *The Catechism of Christian Doctrine;* it was full of questions and answers having to do with moral problems, and I was well acquainted with it.

I had a thought, you see. I wanted to check, and make absolutely sure that the first thing I had done was really a Mortal Sin, after all. There were conditions for this sort of thing, I knew, and it was just possible that I had not fulfilled them, that what I had done was to be classed only as a Venial Sin. If that was true, then I had not held back anything serious in Confession, either; and I had not lied to

God. If that was the case, I was free, free to enjoy life again.

My mother called down to me; what was I doing down there? Shouldn't I be going to bed? I said that I would shut the light out after me, and I found the book.

There were three conditions necessary for the commission of a Mortal Sin, the kind of sin that cut a person off from God, the book said. First, the failure had to involve a grievous matter. I read on for quite a while, but the more I read the more it was clear that sex was always grievous, and that if you had failed in this respect, which was my case, there could be no help from condition number one.

"Sufficient Reflection," was condition number two. I reflected upon whether I had reflected. And I decided that I had. I wished that I had not; I wished that I had just gone on and done it without thinking.

Number three appeared the only hope left; the last thing required was "Full Consent of the Will." There were definitions of Consent from Saint Thomas Aquinas, and some paragraphs on Freedom by theologians with Spanish-sounding names. But when I got finished with it all, I was no better off than if I had gone up to my bedroom, and tried to sleep. I was damned in the cellar as well as in my room. I had still lied to God; only now I was sure of it.

How ridiculous it all was. I knew that I should laugh, but I felt like crying. I put the book back in its dusty place next to the travel volumes, and turned to leave; but as I did so, something strange caught my attention, off in the shadow of the shelves. I was startled; from its shape I did not know what it might be. I went over cautiously to investigate it, and found that it was the old Depression Plant, still sitting in its dish, but protected by newspapers, and placed carefully in the center of a bushel-basket. Someone had grown tired of seeing it on the dining room table, and had put it down there preparatory to throwing it out.

I looked at it. It was growing away there in the dark, without light or air or even water, and with nothing but itself to feed on; it seemed poisonous and hateful, and yet I knew that I was looking into a mirror. What a sublime joke I had become. From the brightest boy in class, to my unreal relationship with Jean Mangan, to the fellow at Isaly's, to the ridiculous sin I had committed; and now to this: down in the cellar with the Depression Plant, arguing with Saint Thomas Aquinas about Everlasting Life, and worrying about whales.

I was too much of something for my own good. I was too much of everything, maybe. I thought too much. I read too much. I daydreamed, and worried about God too much. And in my plan for the salvation of the world I was concerned with many things that any adult could have told me are better left alone. ("For who can draw out Leviathan with a hook?" I want to shout back, now, to that strange theologian of a boy; "And Euroclydron," I want to ask, "—shalt thou play with him as with a bird, and catch him in thy nets?")

I shut the lights off, went up to bed, and fell asleep.

Next day, being Saturday, I got myself cleaned up, and went to church. I knelt at the altar rail to ask for courage; then I joined the long line of sinners waiting to be forgiven. Most of them were little children, younger than I, for I had chosen strategically their Confessor, old Father O'Connell, who was almost too deaf to hear, and too distant to understand. The line slowly bumped its way toward salvation past a steam radiator, making the tinny covering sound out from time to time through the old church; and finally it was my turn.

No dog sick in a corner ever vomited up more violently than I confessed my sins that time. I coughed up my days and ways fiercely, determinedly, in detail, gasping for air between sins to tell everything, *everything*: so that what I had gone through I would never have to go through again.

My hands fastened themselves to the top of the kneeler so that I would not run away, and I told each failure, starting with the bedroom, to the holding back in the confessional, to the many secret thoughts I had had, and ending finally with the crowning sin of disbelief, of having doubted the existence of God.

And old Father O'Connell, who was too distracted to understand the enormity of my guilt, and too concerned with his own special themes to give any thought to mine, waited impatiently for me to be silent. At last I was done, and then he spoke. He talked at some length against going to movies on Sunday; he gave me a light penance, and then he said the words of Absolution. I was free.

I cannot now say what I then felt: lions, harts and leaping does could not have bounded forth from that confining place with more joy than I did. I burst out into the day, and saw that it was afternoon. A gentle May mist was falling, nourishing the lilac trees and honeysuckled lawns of Franklin Road; I was astonished at how lovely rain smelled; it had been raining on the way up, too, but I had not cared. I remember stopping on the wooden steps leading down from the side door of the church. The railing was of course wet with rain; I went over to it and pounded it with my fist, glorying that it was real, and that I could enjoy it. And later on, when the sun did shine, I almost could not stand the beauty of the day. I would go to Holy Communion in the morning with everyone else, and Eternity held no fears for me.

I stopped at the newspaper stand on the corner of Perrysville Avenue and East Street: there were front page pictures of the Pittsburgh contingent of the Bonus Army standing on box-cars in the nation's capitol, and pictures of tombstones with "Andy Mellon" written on them; and there was the news that Father Coughlin had sent the men a check for $5,000, stipulating only that they not allow the virus of International Communism to penetrate their ranks.

I hurried home, for on Saturdays we had a genuine ball-game, on the sand-lot. I rounded the top of Ritchey Street full of anticipation, and triumph, and a pride that I had not felt for a long time.

And there, coming up Ritchey Street on the opposite side-walk was Jean Marie Mangan. She was going up to Confession. Her knees shone whitely and prettily against the edge of her dress as she climbed the hill. What sins could she possibly have to tell?

For a moment I did not know what to do; then I shouted across the rectangular old limestone cobblestones of Ritchey Street a loud and respectful "Hello." It was the closest I ever came to saying what I thought.

For a while it seemed that my God was marching on, with the Bonus Army, under our very windows. But within a few days the names Douglas MacArthur and Dwight Eisenhower became famous; they had routed the men with cavalry and tanks in Washington. The men came streaming home along the railroad tracks to Johnstown and Ambridge and Aliquippa, and I did not know what to think. I found myself standing on the sand-lot, looking out over the roof-tops of Pittsburgh, wondering about it, and about all things.

I had pretty much made up my mind to go to Samarkand, alone; but I had not solved everything. I thought and thought, through the summer, about what had happened. I thought about Pittsburgh, and Shantytown, and the men, and Father Cox, and Old Saint Patrick's Church, and the Grotto of Our Lady of Lourdes. But the more I thought, the more it only seemed clear to me that there were people in

Pittsburgh who believed that Our Lady of Lourdes wanted Andy Mellon taken out and shot. And that finished it; I couldn't get past that for it made me smile, even though I didn't want to. And that's the way it ended, with a smile, and a shake of the head towards Shantytown.

But it is really not over yet. It is years later, and I still have not solved anything. I think of a boy on a dolphin, years ago, riding out toward the edges of a dangerous sea. And I want to warn him, to shout something back at him across the years. "Behold Euroclydon," I want to say; "for he makes the deep sea to boil, and he leaves a path in the waters shining after him. But there is no power on earth that can hold him: small rider, he has broken all our nets."

Winterkill

I HAD NOT BEEN BACK in town long. Maybe a month was all. The work had finally given out for me down at Silver Bow, and I had quit staying around down there when the weather turned cold, and come back to my mother's, on the Bitterroot, to lay up and set my benefits aside for when things got worse.

My mother had her boyfriend then, an old wildcatter named Harley Reeves. And Harley and I did not get along, though I don't blame him for that. He had been laid off himself down near Gillette, Wyoming, where the boom was finished. And he was just doing what I was doing and had arrived there first. Everyone was laid off then. It was not a good time in that part of Montana, nor was it going to be. The two of them were just giving it a final try, both of them in their sixties, strangers together in the little house my father had left her.

So in a week I moved up to town, into a little misery flat across from the Burlington Northern yards, and began to wait. There was nothing to do. Watch TV. Stop in a bar. Walk down to the Clark Fork River and fish where they had built a little park. Just find a way to spend the time. You think you'd like to have all the time be your own, but that is a fantasy. I was feeling my back to the wall then, and didn't know what would happen to me in a week's time, which is a feeling to stay with you and make being cheerful hard. And no one can like that.

I was at the Top Hat having a drink with Little Troy Burnham, talking about the deer season, when a woman who had been sitting at the front of the bar got up and came over to us. I had seen this woman other times in other bars in town. She would be there in the afternoons around three, and then sometimes late at night when I would be cruising back. She danced with some men from the air base, then sat drinking and talking late. I suppose she left with someone finally. She wasn't a bad-looking woman at all. Blond, with wide, dark eyes set out, wide hips, and dark eyebrows. She could've been thirty-four years old, although she could've been forty-four or twenty-four, because she was drinking steady, and steady drink can do both to you, especially to women. But I had thought the first time I saw her: Here's one on the way down. A miner's wife drifted up from Butte, or a rancher's daughter just run off suddenly, which can happen. Or worse. And I hadn't been tempted. Trouble comes cheap and leaves expensive is a way of thinking about that.

"Do you suppose you could give me a light?" the woman said to us. She was standing at our table. Nola was her name. Nola Foster. I had heard that around. She wasn't drunk. It was four o'clock in the afternoon, and no one was there but Troy Burnham and me.

"If you'll tell me a love story, I'd do anything in the world for you," Troy said. It was what he always said to women. He'd do anything in the world for something. Troy sits in a wheelchair due to a smoke jumper's injury, and can't do very much. We had been friends since high school and before. He was always short, and I was tall. But Troy had been an excellent wrestler and won awards in Montana, and I had done little of that, some boxing once was all. We had been living in the same apartments on Ryman Street, though Troy lived there permanently and drove a Checker cab to earn a living, and I was hoping to pass on to something better. "I *would* like a little love story," Troy said, and called out for whatever Nola Foster was drinking.

"Nola, Troy. Troy, Nola," I said and lit her cigarette.

"Have we met?" Nola said, taking a seat and glancing at me.

"At the East Gate. Some time ago," I said.

"That's a very nice bar," she said in a cool way. "But I hear it's changed hands."

"I'm glad to make an acquaintance," Troy said, grinning and adjusting his glasses. "Now let's hear that love story." He pulled up close to the table so that his head and his big shoulders were above the tabletop. Troy's injury had caused him not to have any hips left. There is something there, but not hips. He needs bars and a special seat in his cab. He is both frail and strong at once, though in most ways he gets on like everybody else.

"I *was* in love," Nola said quietly as the bartender set her drink down and she took a sip. "And now I'm not."

"That's a short love story," I said.

"There's more to it," Troy said, grinning. "Am I right about that? Here's cheers to you," he said, and raised his glass.

Nola glanced at me again. "All right. Cheers," she said and sipped her drink.

Two men had started playing a pool game at the far end of the room. They had turned on the table light, and I could hear the balls click and someone say, "Bust'em up, Craft." And then the smack.

"You don't want to hear about that," Nola said. "You're drunk men, that's all."

"We do *too*," Troy said. Troy always has enthusiasm. He could very easily complain, but I have never heard it come up. And I believe he has a good heart.

"What about you? What's your name?" Nola said to me.

"Les," I said.

"Les, then," she said. "You don't want to hear this, Les."

"Yes he does," Troy said, putting his elbows on the table and raising himself. Troy was a little drunk. Maybe we all were a little.

"Why not," I said.

"See? Sure. Les wants more. He's like me."

Nola was a pretty woman, with a kind of dignity to her that wasn't at once so noticeable, and Troy was thrilled by her.

"All right," Nola said, taking another drink.

"What'd I tell you?" Troy said.

"I had really thought he was dying," Nola said.

"Who?" I said.

"My husband. Harry Lyons. I don't use that name now. Someone's told you this story before, haven't they?"

"Not me. Goddamn!" Troy said. "I *want* to hear this story."

I said I hadn't heard it either, though I had heard there was a story.

She took a puff on her cigarette and gave us both a look that said she didn't believe us. But she went on. Maybe she had thought about another drink by then.

"He had this death look. Ca-shit-ic, they call it. He was pale, and his mouth turned down like he could see death. His heart had already gone out once in June, and I had the feeling I'd come in the kitchen some morning and he'd be slumped on his toast."

"How old was this Harry?" Troy said.

"Fifty-three years old. Older than me by a lot."

"That's cardiac alley there," Troy said and nodded at me. Troy has trouble with his own organs now and then. I think they all moved lower when he hit the ground.

"A man gets strange when he's going to die," Nola said in a quiet voice. "Like he's watching it come. Though Harry was still going to work out at Champion's every day. He was an estimator. Plus he watched *me* all the time. Watched to see if I was getting ready, I guess. Checking the insurance, balancing the checkbook, locating the safe-deposit key. All that. Though I would, too. Who wouldn't?"

"Bet your ass," Troy said and nodded again. Troy was taking this all in, I could see that.

"And I admit it, I *was*," Nola said. "I loved Harry. But if he died, where was I going? Was I supposed to die, too? I had to make some plans for myself. I had to think Harry was expendable at some point. To *my* life, anyway."

"Probably that's why he was watching you," I said. "He might not have felt expendable in *his* life."

"I know," Nola said and looked at me seriously and smoked her cigarette. "But I had a friend whose husband killed himself. Went into the garage and left the motor running. And his wife *was not* ready. Not in her mind. She thought he was out putting on brake shoes. And there he was when she went out there. She ended up having to move to Washington, D.C. Lost her balance completely over it. Lost her house, too."

"All bad things," Troy agreed.

"And that just wasn't going to be me, I thought. And if Harry had to get wind of it, well, so be it. Some days I'd wake up and look at him in bed and I'd think, Die, Harry, and quit worrying about it."

"I thought this was a love story," I said. I looked down at where the two men were playing an eight-ball rack. One man was chalking a cue while the other man was leaning over to shoot.

"It's coming. Just be patient, Les," Troy said.

Nola drained her drink. "I'll guarantee it is," she said.

"Then let's hear it," I said. "Get on to the love part."

Nola looked at me strangely then, as if I really did know what she was going to tell, and thought maybe I might tell it first myself. She raised her chin at me. "Harry came home one evening from work, right?" she said. "Just death as usual. Only he said to me, 'Nola, I've invited some friends over, sweetheart. Why don't you go out and get a flank steak at Albertson's.' 'When are they coming?' I said. 'In an hour,' he said. And I thought, An hour! Because he never brought people home. We went to bars, you know. We didn't entertain. But I said, 'All right. I'll go get a flank steak.' And I got in the car and went out and bought a flank steak. I thought Harry ought to have what he wants. If he wants to have friends and steak he ought to be able to. Men, before they die, will want strange things."

"That's a fact, too," Troy said seriously. "I was full dead all four minutes when I hit. And I dreamed about nothing but lobster the whole time. And I'd never even seen a lobster, though I have now. Maybe that's what they serve in heaven." Troy grinned at both of us.

"Well, this wasn't heaven," Nola said and signaled for another drink. "So when I got back, there was Harry with three Crow Indians, in my house, sitting in the living room drinking mai tais. A man and two women. His *friends,* he said. From the plant. He wanted to have his friends over, he said. And Harry was raised a strict Mormon. Not that it matters."

"I guess he had a change of heart," I said.

"That'll happen, too," Troy said gravely. "LDS's aren't like they used to be. They used to be bad, but that's all changed. Though I guess coloreds still can't get inside the temple all the way."

"These three were inside my house, though. I'll just say that. And I'm not prejudiced about it. Leopards with spots, leopards without. All the same to me. But I was nice. I went right in the kitchen and put the flank steak in the oven, put some potatoes in water, got out some frozen peas. And went back in to have a drink. And we sat around and talked for half an hour. Talked about the plant. Talked about Marlon Brando. The man and one of the women were married. He worked with Harry. And the other woman was his sister. Winona. There's a town in Mississippi with the same name. I looked it up. So after a while—all nice and friends—I went in to peel my potatoes. And this other woman, Bernie, came in with me to help, I guess. And I was standing there cooking over a little range, and this Bernie said to me, 'I don't know how you do it, Nola.' 'Do what, Bernie?' I said. 'Let Harry go with my sister like he does and you stay so happy about it. I couldn't ever stand that with Claude.' And I just turned around and looked at her. *Winona is what?* I thought. That seemed so unusual for an Indian. And I just started yelling it. 'Winona, Winona,' at the top of my lungs right at the stove. I just went crazy a minute, I guess. Screaming, holding a potato in my hand, hot. The man came running into the kitchen. Claude Smart Enemy. Claude was awfully nice. He kept me from harming myself. But when I started yelling, Harry, I guess, figured everything was all up. And he and his Winona woman went right out the door. And he didn't get even to the car when his heart went. He had a myocardial infarction right out on the sidewalk at this Winona's feet. I guess he thought everything was going to be just great. We'd all have dinner together. And I'd never know what was what. Except he didn't count on Bernie saying something."

"Maybe he was trying to make you appreciate him more," I said. "Maybe he didn't like being expendable and was sending you a message."

Nola looked at me seriously. "I thought of that," she said. "I thought about that more than once. But that would've been hurtful. And Harry Lyons wasn't a man to hurt you. He was more of a sneak. I just think he wanted us all to be friends."

"That makes sense," Troy said, nodding and looking at me.

"What happened to Winona?" I said.

"What happened to Winona?" Nola took a drink and gave me a hard look. "Winona moved herself to Spokane. What happened to me is a better question."

"Why, you're here with us," Troy said enthusiastically.

"You're doing great. Les and me ought to do as well as you do. Les is out of work. And I'm out of luck. You're doing the best of the three of us, I'd say."

"I wouldn't," Nola said frankly and turned and stared down at the men playing pool.

"What'd he leave you?" I said. "Harry."

"Two thousand," Nola said coldly.

"That's a small amount," I said.

"And it's a sad love story too," Troy said, shaking his head. "You loved him and it ended rotten. That's like Shakespeare."

"I loved him enough," Nola said.

"How about sports. Do you like sports?" Troy said.

Nola looked at Troy oddly then. In his chair Troy doesn't look exactly like a whole man, and sometimes simple things he'll say will seem surprising. And what he'd said then surprised Nola. I have gotten used to it, myself, after all these years.

"Did you want to try skiing?" Nola said and glanced at me.

"Fishing," Troy said, up on his elbows again. "Let's all of us go fishing. Put an end to old gloomy." Troy seemed like he wanted to pound the table. And I wondered when was the last time he had slept with a woman. Fifteen years ago, maybe. And now that was all over for him. But he was excited just to be here and get to talk to Nola Foster, and I wasn't going to be in his way. "No one'll be there now," he said. "We'll catch a fish and cheer ourselves up. Ask Les. He caught a fish."

I had been going mornings in those days, when the *Today* show got over. Just kill an hour. The river runs the middle of town, and I could walk over in five minutes and fish downstream below the motels that are there, and could look up at the blue and white mountains down the Bitter-root, toward my mother's house, and sometimes see the geese coming back up their flyway. It was a strange winter. January was like a spring day, and the Chinook blew down

over us a warm wind from the eastern slopes. Some days
were cool or cold, but many days were warm, and the only
ice you'd see was in the lows where the sun didn't reach.
You could walk right out to the river and make a long cast
to where the fish were deep down in the cold pools. And you
could even think things might turn out better.

Nola looked at me then. The thought of fishing was seem-
ing like a joke to her, I know. Though maybe she didn't
have money for a meal and thought we might buy her one.
Or maybe she'd never even been fishing. Or maybe she
knew that she was on her way to the bottom, where everything is the same, and here was this something different
being offered, and it was worth a try if nothing else.

"Did you catch a big fish, Les," she said.

"Yes," I said.

"See?" Troy said. "Am I a liar? Or am I not?"

"You might be," Nola said. She looked at me oddly then,
but, I thought, sweetly too. "What kind of fish was it?"

"A brown trout. Caught deep, on a hare's ear," I said.

"I don't know what that is," Nola said, and smiled. I
could see that she wasn't minding any of this because her
face was flushed, and she looked pretty then.

"Which?" I said. "A brown trout? Or a hare's ear?"

"That's it," she said.

"A hare's ear is a kind of fly," I said.

"I see," Nola said.

"Let's get out of the bar for once," Troy said loudly,
running his chair backwards and forwards. "We'll go fish,
then we'll have chicken-in-the-ruff. Troy's paying."

"What'll I lose?" Nola said and shook her head. She
looked at both of us, smiling as though she could think of
something that might be lost.

"You got it all to win," Troy said. "Let's just go."

"Sure," Nola said. "Whatever."

And we went out of the Top Hat, with Nola pushing
Troy in his chair and me coming on behind.

On Front Street the evening was as warm as May, though the sun had gone behind the peaks already, and it was nearly dark. The sky was deep beryl blue in the east behind the Sapphires, where the darkness was, but salmon pink above the sun. And we were in the middle of it. Half drunk, trying to be imaginative in how we killed our time.

Troy's Checker was parked in front, and Troy rolled over to it and spun around.

"Let me show you this great trick," he said and grinned. "Get in and drive, Les. Stay there, sweetheart, and watch me."

Nola had kept her drink in her hand, and she stood by the door of the Top Hat. Troy lifted himself off his chair onto the concrete. I got in beside Troy's bars and his raised seat and started the cab with my left hand.

"Ready," Troy shouted. "Ease forward. Ease up."

And I eased the car up.

"Oh my God," I heard Nola say and saw her put her palm to her forehead and look away.

"*Yaah. Ya-hah,*" Troy yelled.

"Your poor foot," Nola said.

"It doesn't hurt me," Troy yelled. "It's just like a pressure." I couldn't see him from where I was.

"I know I've seen it all now," Nola said. She was smiling.

"Back up, Les. Just ease it back again," Troy yelled out.

"Don't do it again," Nola said.

"One time's enough, Troy," I said. No one else was in the street. I thought how odd it would be for anyone to see that, without knowing something in advance. A man running over another man's foot for fun. Just drunks, you'd think, I guess. And be right.

"Sure. Okay," Troy said. I still couldn't see him. But I put the cab back in park and waited. "Help me, sweetheart, now," I could hear Troy say to Nola. "It's easy getting down, but old Troy can't get up again by himself. You have to help him."

And Nola looked at me in the cab, the glass still in her hand. And it was an odd look she gave me, a look that seemed to ask something of me, but I did not know what it was and couldn't answer. And then she put her glass on the pavement and went to put Troy back in his chair.

When we got to the river it was as good as dark, and the river was only a big space you could hear, with the south-of-town lights up behind it, and the three bridges and Champion's paper, downstream a mile. And it was cold now with the sun gone, and I thought there would be fog in before morning.

Troy had insisted on driving with us in the back, as if we'd hired a cab to take us fishing. On the way down he sang a smoke jumper's song, and Nola sat close to me and let her leg be beside mine. And by the time we stopped by the river, below the Lion's Head motel, I had kissed her twice, and knew all that I could do.

"I think I'll go fishing," Troy said from his little raised-up seat in front. "I'm going night fishing. And I'm going to get my own chair out and my rod and all I need. I'll have a time."

"How do you ever change a tire?" Nola said. She was not moving. It was just a question she had. People say all kinds of things to cripples.

Troy whipped around suddenly, though, and looked back at us where we sat on the cab seat. I had put my arm around Nola, and we sat there looking at his big head and big shoulders, below which there was only half a body any good to anyone. "Trust Mr. Wheels," Troy said. "Mr. Wheels can do anything a whole man can." And he smiled at us a crazy man's smile.

"I think I'll just stay in the car," Nola said. "I'll wait for chicken-in-the-ruff. That'll be my fishing."

"It's too cold for ladies anyway now," Troy said gruffly. "Only men. Only men in wheelchairs is the new rule."

I got out of the cab with Troy then and set up his chair and put him in it. I got his fishing gear out of the trunk and strung it up. Troy was not a man to fish flies, and I put a silver dace on his spin line and told him to hurl it far out and let it flow for a time with the current until it was deep, and then to work it, and work it all the way in. I said he would catch a fish with that strategy in five minutes, or ten.

"Les," Troy said to me in the cold dark behind the cab.

"What," I said.

"Do you ever just think of doing a criminal thing sometime? Just do something terrible. Change everything."

"Yes," I said. "I think about that."

Troy had his fishing rod across his chair now, and he was gripping it and looking down the sandy bank toward the dark and sparkling water.

"Why don't you do it?" he said.

"I don't know what I'd choose to do," I said.

"Mayhem," Troy said. "Commit mayhem."

"And go to Deer Lodge forever," I said. "Or maybe they'd hang me and let me dangle. That would be worse than this, I think."

"Okay, that's right," Troy said, still staring. "But *I* should do it, shouldn't I? I should do the worst thing there is."

"No, you shouldn't," I said.

And then he laughed. "Hah. Right. Never do that," he said. And he wheeled himself down toward the river into the darkness, laughing all the way, "Hah, hah, hah."

In the cold cab after that I held Nola Foster for a long time. Just held her with my arms around her, breathing and waiting. From the back window I could see the Lion's Head motel, see the restaurant there that faces the river and that is lighted with candles where people were eating. I could see the WELCOME out front, though not who was welcomed. I could see cars on the bridge going home for the night. And it made me think of Harley Reeves, in my father's little house on the Bitterroot. I thought about him in bed with my mother. Warm. I thought about the faded old tattoo on Harley's shoulder. VICTORY, that said. And I could not connect it easily with what I knew about Harley Reeves, though I thought possibly that he had won a victory of kinds over me just by being where he was.

Nola Foster said, "A man who isn't trusted is the worst thing, you know that, don't you?" I suppose her mind was wandering. She was cold. I could tell by the way she held me. Troy was gone out in the dark now. We were alone, and her skirt had come up a good ways.

"Yes, that's bad," I said, though I could not think at that moment of what trust could mean to me. It was not an issue in my life, and I hoped it never would be. "You're right," I said to make her happy. I felt I could do that.

"What was your name again?"

"Les," I said. "Lester Snow. Call me Les."

"Les Snow," Nola said. "Do you like less snow?"

"Usually I do," I said, and put my hand then where I wanted it most.

"How old are you, Les?" she said.

"Thirty-seven," I said.

"You're an old man."

"How old are you?" I said.

"It's my business, isn't it?"

"I guess it is," I said.

"I'll do this, you know," Nola said, "and not even care about it. Just do a thing. It means nothing more than how I feel at this time. You know? Do you know what I mean, Les?"

"I know it," I said.

"But *you* need to be trusted. Or you aren't anything. Do you know that too?"

We were close to each other. I couldn't see the lights of town or the motel or anything more. Nothing moved.

"I know that, I guess," I said. It was whiskey talking.

"Warm me up then, Les," Nola said. "Warm. Warm."

"You'll get warm," I said.

"I'll think about Florida," she said.

"I'll make you warm," I said.

What I thought I heard at first was a train. So many things can sound like a train when you live near trains. This was a *woo* sound, you would say. Like a train. And I lay and listened for a long time, thinking about a train and its light shining through the darkness along the side of some mountain pass north of there and about something else I don't even remember now. And then Troy came around to my thinking, and I knew then that the *woo* sound had been Troy.

Nola Foster said, "It's Mr. Wheels. He's caught a fish, maybe. Or else drowned."

"Yes," I said.

And I sat up and looked out the window but could see nothing. It had become foggy in just that little time, and tomorrow, I thought, it would be warm again, though it was cold now. Nola and I had not even taken off our clothes to do what we had done.

"Let me see," I said.

I got out and walked into the fog to where I could only see fog and hear the river running. Troy had not made a *woo*ing sound again, and I thought to myself, There is no trouble here. Nothing's wrong.

Though when I walked a ways up the sandy bank, I saw Troy's chair come visible in the fog. And he was not in it, and I couldn't see him. And my heart went then. I heard it go click in my chest. And then I thought, This is the worst. What's happened here will be the worst. And I called out, "Troy. Where are *you*? Call out, now."

And Troy called out, "Here I am, here."

I went for the sound then, ahead of me, which was not out in the river but on the bank. And when I had gone farther, I saw him, out of his chair, of course, on his belly, holding on to his fishing rod with both hands, the line out into the river as though it meant to drag him to the water.

"Help me!" he yelled. "I've got a huge fish. Do something to help me."

"I will," I said. Though I did not see what I could do. I would not dare to take the rod, and it would only have been a mistake to take the line. Never give a straight pull to the fish, is an old rule. So that my only choice was to grab Troy and hold him until the fish was either in or lost, just as if Troy was a part of a rod *I* was fishing with.

I squatted in the cold sand behind him, put my heels down and took up his legs, which felt to me like matchsticks, and began to hold him there away from the water.

But Troy suddenly twisted toward me fiercely. "Turn me loose, Les. Don't be there. Go out. It's snagged. You've got to go out."

"That's crazy," I said. "It's too deep there."

"It's not deep," Troy yelled. "I've got it in close now."

"You're crazy," I said.

"Oh, Christ, Les, go get it. I don't want to lose it."

I looked a moment at Troy's scared face then, in the dark. His glasses were gone off of him. His face was wet. And he had the look of a desperate man, a man who has nothing to hope for but, in some strange way, everything in the world to lose.

"Stupid. This is stupid," I said, because it seemed to me to be. But I got up, walked to the edge and stepped out into the cold water.

It was at least a month then before the runoff would begin in the mountains, and the water I stepped in then was cold and painful as broken glass, though the wet parts of me numbed at once, and my feet just felt like bricks bumping the bottom.

Troy had been wrong all the way about the depth. Because when I stepped out ten yards, keeping touch of his line with the back of my hand, I had already gone above my knees, and on the bottom I felt large rocks, and there was a loud rushing around me that suddenly made me afraid.

Though when I had gone five more yards, and the water was on my thighs and hurting, I hit the snag Troy's fish was hooked to, and I realized then I had no way at all to hold a fish or catch it with my numbed hands. And that all I could really hope for was to break the snag and let the fish slip down into the current and hope Troy could bring it in, or that I could go back and beach it.

"Can you see it, Les?" Troy yelled out of the dark. "Goddammit."

"It isn't easy," I said, and I had to hold the snag then to keep my balance. My legs had gone numb. And I thought: This might be the time and the place I die. What an odd place it is. And what an odd reason for it to happen.

"Hurry up," Troy yelled.

And I wanted to hurry. Except when I ran the line as far as where the snag was, I felt something there that was not a fish and not the snag but something else entirely, some thing I thought I recognized, though I am not sure why. A man, I thought. This is a man.

Though when I had reached farther into the snag branches and woods scruff, deeper into the water, what I felt was an animal. With my fingers I touched its cold, hard rib-side, its legs, its short, slick coat. I felt to its neck and head and touched its nose and teeth, and it was a deer, though not a big deer, not even a yearling. And I knew when I found where Troy's silver dace had gone up in the neck flesh, that he had hooked the deer already snagged here, and that he had pulled himself out of his chair trying to work it free.

"What is it? I know it's a big brown. Don't tell me, Les, don't even tell me."

"I've got it," I said. "I'll bring it in."

"Sure, hell yes," Troy said out of the fog.

And it was not so hard to work the deer off the snag brush and float it up free. Though once I did, it was dangerous to get turned around in the current with numb legs, and hard to keep from going down, and I had to hold onto the deer itself to keep balance enough to heave myself toward the slow water and the bank. And I thought, as I did, that in the Clark Fork many people drown doing less dangerous things than I am doing now.

"Throw it way far up," Troy shouted, when he could see me. He had righted himself on the sand and was sitting up like a little doll. "Get it way up safe," he said to me.

"It's safe," I said. I had the deer beside me, floating, but I knew Troy couldn't see.

"What did I catch?" Troy yelled.

"Something unusual," I said, and with effort I hauled the little deer up on the sand a foot, dropped it, and put my cold hands up under my arms. I heard a car door close back where I had come from up the riverbank.

"What is that?" Troy said and put his hand out to touch the deer's dark side. He looked up at me. "I can't see without my glasses."

"It's a deer," I said.

Troy moved his hand around on the deer, then looked at me again in a painful and bewildered way.

"What's it?" he said.

"A deer," I said. "You caught a dead deer."

Troy looked back at the little deer then for a moment and stared at it as if he did not know what to say about it. And sitting on the wet sand, in the foggy night, he all at once looked scary to me, as though it was him who had washed up there and was finished. "I don't see it," he said and sat there. And I said nothing.

"It's what you caught," I said finally. "I thought you'd want to see it."

"It's crazy, Les," he said. "Isn't it?" And he smiled at me in a wild, blind-eyed way.

"It's unusual," I said.

"I never shot a deer before."

"I don't believe you shot this one," I said.

And he smiled again, but then suddenly he gasped back a sob, something I had never seen before. "Goddammit," he said. "Just goddammit."

"It's an odd thing to catch," I said, standing above him in the cold, grimy fog.

"I can't change a fucking tire," he said and sobbed again. "But I'll catch a fucking deer with my fucking fishing rod."

"Not everyone can say that," I said.

"Why would they want to?" He looked up at me crazy again, and broke his spinning rod into two pieces with only his hands. And I knew he must've been drunk still, because I was still drunk a little, and that by itself made me want to cry. And we were there for a time just silent.

"Who killed a deer?" Nola said. She had come behind me in the cold night and was looking. I had not known, when I heard the car door, if she wasn't walking back up to town. But it was too cold for that, and I put my arm around her because she was shivering. "Did Mr. Wheels kill it?" she said.

"It drowned," Troy said.

"And why is that?" Nola said and pushed closer to me to be warm, though that was all.

"They get weak, and they fall over," I said. "It happens in the mountains. This one fell in the water and couldn't get up."

"So a gimp man can catch it on a fishing rod in a shitty town," Troy said and gasped with bitterness again. Real bitterness. The worst I have ever heard from any man, and I have heard bitterness voiced, though it was a union matter then.

"Maybe it isn't so bad," Nola said.

"Hah!" Troy said loudly from the wet ground. "Hah, hah, hah." And I wished that I had never shown him the deer, wished I had spared him that, though the river's rushing came up then and snuffed his sound right out of hearing, and drew it away from us into the foggy night beyond all accounting.

Nola and I pushed the deer back into the river while Troy watched, and then we all three drove up into town and ate chicken-in-the-ruff at the Two-Fronts, where the lights were bright and they cooked the chicken fresh for you. I bought a jug of wine and we drank that while we ate, though no one talked much. Each of us had done something that night. Something different. That was plain enough. And there was nothing to talk about to make any difference.

When we were finished, we walked outside and I asked Nola where she would like to go. It was only eight o'clock, and there was no place to go but to my little room. She said she wanted to go back to the Top Hat, that she had someone to meet there later, and there was something about the band that night that she liked. She said she wanted to dance.

I told her I was not much for dancing, and she said fine. And when Troy came out from paying, we said goodbye, and she shook my hand and said that she would see me again. Then she and Troy got in the Checker and drove away together down the foggy street, leaving me alone, where I didn't mind being at all.

For a long time I just walked then. My clothes were wet, but it wasn't so cold if you kept moving, though it stayed foggy. I walked to the river again and across on the bridge and then a long way down into the south part of town, on a wide avenue where there were houses with little porches and little yards, all the way, until it became commercial, and bright lights lit the drive-ins and car lots. I could've walked then, I thought, clear to my mother's house twenty miles away. But I turned back, and walked the same way, only on the other side of the street. Though when I got near the bridge again, I came past the senior citizen recreation where there were soft lights on inside a big room, and I could see through a window in the pinkish glow, old people dancing across the floor to a record player that played in a corner. It was a rumba or something like a rumba that was being played, and the old people were dancing the box step, smooth and graceful and courteous, moving across the linoleum like real dancers, their arms on each other's shoulders like husbands and wives. And it pleased me to see that. And I thought that it was too bad my mother and father could not be here now, too bad they couldn't come up and dance and go home happy, and me to watch them. Or even for my mother and Harley Reeves, the wildcatter, to do that. It didn't seem like too much to wish for. Just a normal life other people had.

I stood and watched them awhile, and then I walked back home across the river. Though for some reason I could not sleep that night, and simply lay in bed with the radio turned on to Denver, and smoked cigarettes until it was light. Of course I thought about Nola Foster, that I didn't know where she lived, though for some reason I thought she might live in Frenchtown, out Route 20 west, near the pulp plant. Not far. Never-never Land, they called that. And I thought about my father, who had once gone to Deer Lodge prison for stealing hay from a friend, and had never recovered from it, though that meant little to me now.

And I thought about the matter of trust. That I would always lie if it would save someone an unhappiness. That was easy. And that I would rather a person mistrusted me than dislike me. Though still, I thought, you could always trust me to act a certain way, to be a place, or to say a thing if it ever were to matter. You could predict within human reason what I'd do, that I would not, for example, commit a vicious crime, trust that I would risk my own life for you if I knew it meant enough. And as I lay in the gray light, smoking, while the refrigerator clicked and the switcher in the Burlington Northern yard shunted cars and made their couplings, I thought that though my life at that moment seemed to have taken a bad turn and paused, it still meant something to me as a life, and that before long it would start again in some promising way.

I know I must've dozed a little, because I woke suddenly and there was the light. Earl Nightengale was on the radio, and I heard a door close. It was that that woke me.

I knew it would be Troy, and I thought I would step out and meet him, fix coffee for us before he went to bed and slept all day, the way he always did. But when I stood up I heard Nola Foster's voice. I could not mistake that. She was drunk. And she was laughing about something. "Mr. Wheels," she said. Mr. Wheels this, Mr. Wheels that. Troy was laughing. And I heard them come in the little entry, heard Troy's chair bump the sill. And I waited to see if they would knock on my door. And when they didn't, and I heard Troy's door shut and the chain go up, I thought that we had all had a good night finally. Nothing had happened that hadn't turned out all right. None of us had been harmed. And I put on my pants, then my shirt and shoes, turned off my radio, went to the kitchen, where I kept my fishing rod, and with it went out into the warm, foggy morning, using just this once the back door, the quiet way, so as not to see or be seen by anyone.

ELLEN GILCHRIST

The Young Man

THIS IS A STORY about an old lady who ordered a young man from an L. L. Bean catalog. He was a nice young man with wide shoulders and a worried smile. He had on a tweed coat and dark tan pants and a nice-looking tie with little squiggly things all over it. His fingernails were clean and his hair neatly combed. He liked to work but he was also a good companion on trips. His table manners were excellent but not noticeable. He liked to talk but knew how to let the other person have their turn. Mrs. Bradlee never did get around to asking him what his profession was, his line of work. There never did seem to be a polite way to ask.

All of Mrs. Bradlee's friends were getting young men. You could hardly find four for bridge anymore at the Recess Club. Fanny Hawkins had even started dressing like her young man, flat shoes and work pants. Carrie Hatcher pretended her young man was a chauffeur. All they did was drive around talking about themselves. Elsie Whitfield stayed on the coast with hers, they went fishing. It made Mrs. Bradlee sick at her stomach to think of it. One night she dreamed a big Greyhound bus pulled up in front of the old courthouse on State Street and all these young men got out and started spreading out all over Jackson, moving out in all directions. Like a web that had fallen over the world.

Mrs. Bradlee wasn't having anything to do with it. They weren't eating dinner at her house. I've seen enough, she told herself. I've had enough to contend with. Mrs. Bradlee was a widow. She had buried a son from an automobile accident and a husband from smoking cigarettes. All I want to do from now on is live a normal life she told her remaining children. So whatever you do don't tell me about it. Just come over on Sunday after church while you're still covered up.

You shouldn't live alone, her friends were always telling Mrs. Bradlee. She still lived in her house on Lakefront Drive, with all her rooms. They wanted her to get an apartment where they were, at Westchester Arms, or Dunleith Court or Dunsinae Towers. Well, she wasn't going to move into an apartment. She wasn't joining the herd. She had been raised in the country. She had seen one cow lead the rest to water. Still, it was getting lonely in the big stone house. If only it could be like it used to be, with her friends coming over for cards. They had even started bringing the young men to Saint James. Right up to the prayer rail, and beyond. Alece Treadway was sending hers to divinity school.

It was too much. In the past Mrs. Bradlee had been known as the leader. She had been the first to cut her hair at college, the first to have a white cook, the first to get a facelift (when the time came), the first to visit behind the Iron Curtain. When August, her husband, was still alive. Now, with their craze for young men, the crowd had left her behind.

It was all so, well, so messy. And the young men themselves, well, she hated to cast stones, but they were messy too. Well, they were. They wore open collar sport shirts and tennis sneakers and barely cut their hair. It was too much. It was just too much. Mrs. Bradlee's knitting needles clicked like a thousand crickets. She was alone in her living room. A beautiful sunset was covering the lake with her favorite shades of blue and pink. Elvie Howard had bowed out of their Wednesday night Canasta game, now that she had her swimming pool maintenance friend. He has a degree in Philosophy, she told Mrs. Bradlee, from the East. It's television, Mrs. Bradlee decided. That's where they got the ideas. She switched off her own and went into the library to read.

A stack of catalogs was on a table by the windowseat. She began flipping through them, thinking of ordering some clothes for the grandchildren for Christmas. She took a piece of chocolate from a dish and began to nibble on it, looking at the elegant clothes and shoes and handcarved decoys, the scarves and ties and stacks of well-made shirts. One model began to catch her eye. He was in several different catalogs. The best picture was on page sixteen of the L. L. Bean catalog. He had such neat hair, his smile was so, well, just right, not too smiley, just enough so you would know he was friendly. His hands were in his pockets. He was standing so tall and straight. I ought to order him, she thought. Laughing to herself out loud. She ate another piece of chocolate. Then another. Hello, she said, to the photograph. What's your name?

It was growing dark outside. She pushed a light switch and carried the catalog over to a desk and sat down and took an order blank out of the back and began to fill it in. *One,* she wrote, page *16,* number *331,* color, *white,* she paused at where to fill in the amount. *$10,000,* she wrote and added her Merrill Lynch Visa Card Number. There, that should be about right. She folded the order blank in halves, stuck it into a self-addressed envelope and carried it across the room to the marble table before the fireplace. She dropped it on a silver salver. Here, Mr. Postman, she said, as if she were a child playing at things, take this letter to the warehouse.

The phone was ringing in the hall. The cook was calling her to dinner.

In the morning the envelope was gone. "Have you seen an envelope I left in the library?" she said to the maid. "Well, yes, I did," the girl said. "I mailed it for you. In the morning mail."

"Oh, you can't mail that," Mrs. Bradlee said. "It was a joke. Those people will think I'm crazy when they open that. They'll say, here's a woman in Mississippi who's lost her mind."

"What was it, ma'am?" the maid said.

"I ordered something they don't sell," she said. The two of them laughed together at that. Mrs. Bradlee liked the little maid. An octaroon named Rivers, a sweet girl who was always neat and clean and smelled good.

It was a week later when the young man came. It was nine in the morning. A Sunday morning. Mrs. Bradlee had been up and dressed for an hour, enjoying the fall colors out the windows. She saw him coming up the walk. "You ordered me," he said. "And here I am."

"Go away," she said.

"I can't," he said. "I belong here now. You asked for me. I don't have any other place to be."

"Have you had breakfast," she asked.

"No," he said.

"Come in," she said. "I will feed you." It was warm in the breakfast room, filled with morning sunlight. "Do you mind if I take off my coat?" he said. "Oh, no," she answered. "Here, let me take it for you." She took the lovely tweed coat and laid it across an empty chair. It was the cook's day off. She fixed eggs and toast and juice. When he was finished he laid his fork and knife neatly along the edge of the plate. "If you'll excuse me now," he said. "I would like to use your bathroom."

She led the way to the guest room. When he returned she suggested that they go to church. "Mr. Biggs, our choir director, has a special musicale this morning. After morning prayer. You might enjoy that."

"It will be fine," he said. "I'm sure I'll think it's just right." You should have seen the eyes when Mrs. Bradlee walked in with him, walked right up front to her regular pew and he helped her in and pulled down the prayer bench and knelt beside her. Thank you, she heard herself pray, you know I deserved this. The music was grand, clear and cold as water running over stones. The whole church and all its people melded together by music, one big melodic pyramid. Afterwards, they stood outside and Mrs. Bradlee introduced him all around. His name was Larry Bean. "Bean," Carrie Hatcher said. "I've heard that name."

"We're from England," he said. "The British Isles."

In the afternoon they took naps in their rooms, then went for a walk around the grounds, down to the lake, and back to the house. He walked at just the right rate of speed, not running ahead of her all the time like August did, saying Can't you keep up, if you didn't talk so much you could keep up with me. Larry didn't mind how much Mrs. Bradlee talked. He was interested in everything she said.

"How long are you staying?" she asked finally. It was after dinner. They were having coffee in the den. It seemed like the proper thing to say.

"How long did you want me for?" he asked. He was looking straight at her out of his dark blue eyes. He was looking at her as if there were no wrong answers.

"Let me think about it," she said. "I'm still getting used to the idea."

"Fine," he said. "Whatever you say."

"Where would you go if you left here? Where else would you be?"

"I wouldn't be," he said. "There is only here."

"And you don't mind," she said.

"Why should I mind," he answered. "That's the way it is."

"I'm going to bed now," she said. "I need to sleep."

"Goodnight then," he said. "I'll see you in the morning."

In the morning it was Monday. She dressed before she went downstairs. They had breakfast. "Now you should go to work," she said. "It's Monday morning."

"Fine," he said. "I'll be back at five-thirty."

"Take the blue car," she said. "I don't use it."

"I will," he said. "I like cars to be blue. It's my favorite color." After he was gone Mrs. Bradlee talked on the phone all morning. All her friends called her, one by one. What's he like, they asked. He likes blue, she answered. His favorite color is blue. Go fishing with us, Elsie Whitfield said. We might, Mrs. Bradlee answered. I'll have to see. Do you want to? she asked him later. I don't know, he said. Do you? I don't think so, she said. It's so messy. Find a nice way to tell them, he said. Don't hurt their feelings.

Don't you need some other clothes, she said. You might grow tired of that coat. That will be nice, he said. We'll go shopping at the Mall.

Many days went by. Many weeks. Christmas came and went. They gave each other gifts. He gave her a bracelet with her name inside. She gave him a bundle of fatwood sticks she ordered from Maine and a tiny sled with a gold watch inside. He put it on. His wrist was so perfect. The hair lay so softly along the flesh. Mrs. Bradlee drew in her breath. For a moment she wanted to kiss his hand. God is love, she thought, and reached out and touched him instead. We might go to Switzerland for a month, she said. That would be nice, he answered. I think that would be perfect.

In January the rain fell and the Pearl River rose and the cold came and stayed. It got into Mrs. Bradlee's bones. She felt tired even in the mornings. Her appetite was not good. When she passed Larry in the hall she sighed. He was there every morning. He was there every afternoon. Every Friday she filled the blue car up with gasoline. Every month the gas bill came. Every morning after breakfast he disappeared into the guest room. It made her sick at her stomach to think what he did in there.

She began to be cold to him. She was quiet when they went on walks. She stopped telling him everything. After all, what had he ever told her? She was giving him all her stories. In return, all he knew was blue. Blue skies, blue, blue, blue.

"I think you should play the piano," she told him one evening. "It would be a good idea for you to play."

"I'm not a piano player," he said. "That isn't what you asked for."

"You could learn couldn't you? You could take lessons."

"I'll try," he said. "I'll be glad to try."

"It should sound like this," she said. She took a Mozart sonata out of its cover and put it on the record player. It was sonata number 13 in B major, played by Wanda Landowska. "But that's a woman playing," he said.

"It doesn't matter," Mrs. Bradlee said. "It's all the same thing."

He wasn't any good at the piano. He took lessons after work for three months but nothing happened. His hands were better in his pockets. His hands were better taking the Maine fatwood and using it to light the library fires at night. They were nice laying his knife and fork across his plate after meals. They were too large for the piano or too stiff or too short. Something was wrong. You're disappointed aren't you, he said at last. Yes, she answered, to tell the truth I am. I think you will have to leave soon. It isn't a good idea any more. You will have to find somewhere else to go.

How long should I stay, he asked. I don't know the right amount of time.

Until Easter weekend, she said. That should be about right.

Maundy Thursday came. They met for breakfast without speaking of it. He looked pale. Eat, she said. You should eat before your journey.

On Good Friday they went to communion. He looks tired, Fanny Hawkins said to her. He looks like he needs a rest.

On Holy Saturday he walked all around the house, all day, out into the yard, and down along the river. He looked very beautiful, and light. He had not gone into the guest room after breakfast. He had barely eaten anything at all. Mrs. Bradlee was beginning to enjoy him again. He seemed so light, so easy to support.

Perhaps I'll have him stay till summer she thought, watching his progress across the yard. He was moving toward a line of dogwood trees set against the horizon. Three trees against a blue sky. Yes, I will tell him we will think it over.

The phone rang. It was the refrigerator repairman. What a time to call, she told him. Come Monday. Don't worry about it now. It broke her concentration. She went back to her afghan. She was knitting an afghan to sell at a church bazaar. When Larry came in he walked by without speaking. He did not come down to dinner. I'll talk to him later, she thought. The meal was heavy. She drank too much wine and fell asleep earlier than she expected.

In the morning she went to find him. Of course he was not there. She looked all over the house. She looked in all the closets. She looked in the basement and the wine cellar and the attic. She went out into the garage and looked in the blue car. She went to the guest room. She stood in the door. There was nothing there. The door to the guest room powder room was open. I could look in there, she thought. But I'm not going to.

She went out into the hall and sat down on the stairs. She listened for the sound of footsteps. She thought about the stars. She said the alphabet over and over to herself. It was a trick she had practiced as a child to pass the time. After awhile she went down to the library and got out the new catalogs and began to look through them. I might get a young woman this time, she thought. It was a gay thought. How brave they would all say. A young woman with all the things that can go wrong. I would like a tall one with a long waist she decided. Long legs and a long waist. A singing voice. Piano skills.

A Sounding Brass

IT WAS ONE of those hot Augusts in southern Georgia when the days are especially long and the nights rise up softly out of the ground almost without any notice, until suddenly it is late, ten o'clock, and the children are still outside. But they had not noticed the dark had come, had settled onto the objects around them. And Ginny, too, was surprised at how the night had crept up.

"Come on in," she called to the children, and they ran to the kitchen door where light poured like a pathway across the yard. They raced to the refrigerator, and Jay grabbed his sister's shirt to hold her back, then touched the refrigerator door twice, making it known that he had won. Nell began a long plea, and Jay looked to his mother to judge whether or not he would be reprimanded.

Nell was nine and always on the verge of tears. Ginny put her hand on the little girl's back and told her to take a bath, that the tub was already full. Nell jerked away and looked at her mother with the expression of someone who has been asked to sell everything.

Jay was twelve. He walked with a swagger identical to his father's. Ginny knew he felt the need to take his father's place in the household and that he had felt it since William's death. She tried to relieve him of it.

"What's the matter?" he asked his mother, deciding to take the reprimand. He had made a sandwich of meats and cheese with mustard spilling out all sides.

Ginny thought about the resilience of children, their natural ability for self-preservation, and how at a certain age that ability seems to be forgotten or overrun by other things. And you begin to wonder if those things will end or if they will end you.

"What's the matter?" He wanted to get it over with.

"Nothing," said Ginny, seeing mustard form at the corners of his mouth.

In the last few months Jay had grown taller than his mother, and he liked to kiss the top of her head to prove his height. He leaned now to kiss where her hair parted in the middle. Ginny wiped the mustard from his mouth with her thumb, two quick efficient swipes, the way she had done when he was three. She felt sure she had some in her hair. Jay sat at the table.

"Lemuel called," Ginny said, and Jay turned to her, not knowing what to ask.

"What'd he say?"

"He wants to come here for a visit." Ginny brought him a glass of milk. "On Saturday." It seemed a question.

"I'd like to see him," said Jay.

Neither spoke for a moment, and Ginny pictured Lemuel, the old man who had stood at the back door that morning with his paper and his odd dry look.

Ginny, William, and the children had left for vacation in March. They were to spend two weeks on the coast in a rented house. The house was spacious with a huge porch built on stilts. It faced the sea and was on a strip of private beach. There were no trees in the yard, but scraggly bushes poked out of the sand, and Ginny guessed that was the limit of their growth.

William had driven all night, in a hurry to begin the vacation and not able to consider it begun until they reached their destination. When they arrived, the children preferred the crowds further down the beach and went looking for friends. But Ginny and William loved the privacy. They loved their midnight swims that ended on the sand, then in the outside shower and then on the bedroom floor. As she looked back on that time, she felt glad to have had those days as their last.

Each morning at the beach Ginny rose earlier than the others. She liked to fix breakfast without the need for hurry and organization that her regular mornings demanded. She spooned coffee into the heavy black percolator that came with the house, and placed it squarely on the eye of the stove.

She heard four quick shots from the woods across the street, and could see from the kitchen window two young boys with guns. She wanted to call out to them "Be careful" or something equally protective, but decided not to. She slipped off her shoes to walk on the beach. Returning finally to the house with its fresh-perked-coffee smell, she felt as though she were a guest.

William would usually be sitting at the table when she finished her walk. But this morning she stood at the stove and wondered how late he would sleep. A scratching at the door alarmed her. As she turned around, a man mumbled something and picked up the morning paper to hand to her.

"Pardon?" Ginny asked. She did not want the paper, but reached for her purse anyway. He waved his hand to indicate he didn't want money and said he lived two doors down. He pointed in the direction of the sun.

Ginny could not tell how old he was, but suspected he was not as old as he looked. His hair was white-gray and his face, though lined, was not wrinkled. There was a dryness about him. His skin and hair and voice were raspy. She thanked him, and since he did not turn to leave, she thanked him again, with a finality that sounded almost rude. Then she asked him if he would like a cup of coffee with her, and motioned for him to sit in a porch chair.

He said his name was Lemuel Watkins, and he sat in the biggest, most comfortable chair. In the distance they could hear sirens. Ginny wondered what made her feel apprehensive and decided it was the suddenness of the man's appearance. She offered him cream and sugar.

When she sat down, he leaned toward her. "It's about your husband," he said in a grave voice.

William had heard the shots from the woods across the street and had not been able to return to sleep. Ginny was out walking. He dressed and went to the woods, seeing two boys about Jay's age, maybe younger. They were shooting at wood larks and squirrels, not hitting much of anything, but not caring either. He warned them about pointing the guns toward the house, then asked where they were staying. They said with their grandfather, Lemuel.

As one of the boys stepped foward, he tripped on a twisted root and the gun threw itself forward, straight at William's chest. The boy tried to catch it, but in doing so pulled the trigger. It fired and hit William, one hard, thorough thud, and he fell. The boys ran to their grandfather.

Lemuel called the police and the hospital before he came to tell Ginny. He had hurried, going with quick, frantic motions from William's body to the telephone and then to Ginny. Though when he reached the screen door and saw Ginny standing inside, he moved like a stupid beast from another age.

He told it all to her as the boys had told him. And she ran to find William. His look of bewilderment was still evident. He lay with his long body crumpled over his legs. One arm hung outward as if he were reaching. For that boy, probably, Ginny thought.

"He was reaching to keep that boy from falling," she said out loud, then reached down to move William to a more comfortable position. She looked around wondering where the two boys were.

"They're at home," Lemuel said, as though reading her thoughts.

Ginny did not want to look again at William lying there, so she turned and searched the horizon. She was glad Lemuel was with her, but she blamed him too. Not for the death exactly, but for bringing the news and for his connection to her now. And as she talked she began to shout accusations which she needed to pin on someone. And Lemuel took each one, his head bowed, but sometimes his body would swell up with indignation, and he would say a word or two in defense; but mostly he took it. So that when Ginny was through (her wild arms gesturing, her eyes drained of all their resistance), she turned to see the street full of people and ambulances, and at that moment she blamed them all.

She did not blame them long, not the people, nor the two boys. But for months, even after she had grown to know and love Lemuel, she kept in her mind the image of the old man at the screen door, associating him with her loss.

She walked away from the woods and toward the house where her children still slept. Her feet plodded with assurance and her body followed where they led. Lemuel helped them pack the car. It took all day, and they arrived at home one week from the day they had started their vacation.

Ginny thought of how she had gotten into bed that night, slipping between the cold sheets as if she had to be careful not to spill anything. She felt that if one drop spilled, one drop of what she felt, everything would pour out and she might not have anything left. So she lay flat, looking into the darkness of her room, sightless and infinite. And when her grief came, it came as the sound of a cello, or a bassoon.

When Ginny went upstairs, Nell sat in the middle of her bed eating potato chips. She wore a towel piled high on her head and only her pajama bottoms. She had surrounded herself with objects she chose each night, arranging them in a certain way on her bed, things she could count or handle or look at before sleeping. She rubbed the smooth stomach of a silver-and-bronze fish brought to her by her father a few years ago. The head of the fish was silver and the body bronze, with gills carved in delicate streaks along the sides. The fish had its mouth open, and its strange lips curved as if it were about to drink. Nell loved wearing it around her neck, rubbing its icy, polished head. She loved to put her finger over its mouth, or to lift the mouth to her eye, then to Ginny's eye, its small hollow body so dark that they could not see anything.

Ginny lifted the towel and Nell's hair fell wet and stringy to her shoulders. They combed out the knots and Nell pulled up the covers over her legs, leaving her chest exposed. Her tiny-nippled breasts had barely begun to swell. Ginny pulled a package of cookies from her pocket. Nell unwrapped them, ate two, then put the wrapper into a drawer filled with other papers and wrappers she could not throw away.

"It wasn't fair," Nell said, almost whispering.

"What wasn't?"

"That Jay pulled my shirt and kept me from winning. I would've won."

"I know," said Ginny, and the recognition and agreement seemed to be enough.

"Lemuel's coming on Saturday," Ginny finally said.

Nell seemed glad, but reserved her gladness until she saw what her mother wanted.

"It'll be good to see him, don't you think?" Ginny picked things off the bed and placed them on Nell's shelf.

"Yeah," said Nell, but motioned with her hands. "Not there. Don't put that there. I always put that on the table and the fish on the bottom shelf by the harmonica."

"Oh." Ginny wondered what peculiar order Nell saw for this shelf.

"And the books go at the top," she added with obvious pleasure. Then she spoke suddenly, feeling permission to show enthusiasm. "When will he get here?"

"We'll pick him up at the train on Saturday."

Nell wanted to see Lemuel, though they had seen him in May. Both children had asked about the old man, and in May Nell had asked with such unyielding urgency that Ginny decided to go back to the shore. Nell seemed to think that if they went back, she might find her father again; and Ginny had to admit that she felt the same way herself. No one knew what Jay thought.

Ginny did not call Lemuel to tell him they were coming, so she went first by herself to his house. She rang the door-bell. The bell did not have a bell-like sound, but an uneven rasp that suggested the sound her foot would make against the grainy concrete. The footsteps she heard approaching the door were slow and deliberate, and she was afraid she might not recognize him.

The door was of sliding glass, and he looked at her through it for a moment before opening it. They shared certain features: high cheekbones and thick hair, his lighter now with gray, but still thick. He slid open the glass, and Ginny's voice broke into harsh accusation. She had not meant to.

His eyes were rheumy and his clothes carried the odor of milk. He said her name, his faced fixed upon hers as if he were reading a book; but when she shouted at him his hand drew up and hit her cheek, a quick, bold slap that had been working in his arm. The arm drew up mechanically, knowing what it had planned to do, but his face held no anger.

Ginny, right then, moved to put her arms under his open sweater and around to his skinny back. The slap had hardly been felt. But Lemuel still looked at his hand in the air, and Ginny wondered if he might hit her again. She laid her cheek, which was stinging now, on his shoulder. The coarse wool of his sweater soothed her.

She and the children stayed three days and spent most of their time with Lemuel. Lemuel told how his grandsons had not visited and that the youngest (the one who tripped and fired the shot) might not be all right for a long while. But he loved having Ginny's children there. Jay and Nell loved it too. And even though Ginny could not enter into their play, she felt relieved at their happiness.

Jay was already in bed. He would not call his mother to tell him good night anymore. The nightly ritual of being tucked into bed was too juvenile for him now. But he seemed pleased when Ginny knocked at his door and asked permission to come in. She told him good night in an offhand way, and kissed him while straightening the covers. When she turned out the light, she thanked him for letting her come in, and he called to her through the dark, "Any time."

A summer rain drummed suddenly against the roof and trees. Ginny could hear the thunder, but the pounding felt as if it were going on inside her. A strong, washing kind of rhythm. As she listened, her skin seemed to rise, come alive, the blood pulsing down the seconds, not as if she were losing them, just feeling how they moved through her. And at the height of the moment when everything around her was attuned to the pounding rhythm of the rain, she became alarmed at how alone she was.

She undressed and felt cold, not wanting the warmth of her robe or the blanket at the foot of the bed, but needing another warmth. She slipped her nightgown over her head and looked at herself in the mirror. She wondered how she looked to men.

A week ago there had been a party. Ginny had met someone there. She somehow found it ludicrous that her friends thought she needed male companionship, indeed maybe was even desperate for it. Then she wondered if maybe they were right. She found she did not know how to be with men anymore.

He was adept at words. Each remark indicated that she meant more to him than other people he knew, seeking to establish a bond which had not had time to develop. He did not kiss her then, but when he did, later, she tried to think of what he had been saying or whether or not she had answered him, because she had been tracing with her eyes his hairline which jagged back slightly. Probably farther than it had years ago, and she wondered how old he was, hoping he was older than she.

The kiss he gave was long and practiced, and she returned it with what he later described as a "writhing motion," saying he had never kissed anyone before who writhed. But at that moment, he said nothing.

She felt chilled to the bone and sat down. Then she rubbed her arms, an instinct, a response that gave her the warmth she needed. And she wondered if other people did this, rubbed their arms at the right time and found comfort.

When they brought Lemuel home from the train, Nell took his hand and led him to her room. Jay followed, talking to Lemuel's back. Lemuel nodded to him.

"Let Lemuel sit down," said Ginny, but he said it was all right.

Lemuel's face was thin and his arms hung long. He had the appearance of bending. Nell showed him the tiny fish, letting him look into its mouth and turn it with his hands. Jay talked and boasted with a healthy, child's honesty. Lemuel encouraged him. And Ginny thought of how much like a grandfather this man was to them. She attributed their closeness to the sharing of an irrevocable event; still, when she thought of it she was amazed.

The next morning Jay asked Lemuel to come with him into the woods. He wanted to take him to a tree that stood deep in the woods and could not be seen from the house. The trunk of the tree rose up straight, then veered sharply horizontal before rising again. It looked as if someone had tried to knock it down and failed. The tree had absorbed the blow. There was a knob at the place where it curved upward again, and the knob had a look of force, as if great strength had been focused in that one place. Jay said it looked like an elbow.

There was bark around the lower half, so that when you stood next to it, it looked the same as the other trees, but when you looked up, you could see where the bark quit growing, and underneath a white wood shone, and it looked even whiter in winter. As the tree got higher, it grew thinner and whiter, like a bone; and the leaves that grew, grew high at the top where the pith flowered into leaves. Jay asked Lemuel what made the elbow part turn like that, and Lemuel said that something happened to it when it was young. Jay asked if that could happen again, further up, and when Lemuel looked up he said No.

"The children seem all right," Lemuel told Ginny as he sat at the kitchen table, their first time alone.

"Yes." Ginny was putting breakfast dishes in the cupboard.

"And you? How are you?"

"I'm all right too." Her voice sounded brittle. "Or will be."

Lemuel took a dish from her hand and led her to the table. She sat down quickly, then he sat, but it was a moment before he spoke.

"When I was a boy in Kentucky," he began, and it got Ginny's attention, "I met an immigrant family from Poland. They came to town in the springtime and set up house on a hillside near the railroad tracks. The man was hardworking and found a job at the mill. His wife took in ironing for several families, including mine. So I'd been inside the house to pick up the starched shirts and the smooth dresses. The house always smelled like fresh-baked bread." Ginny looked at him bewildered, though attentive.

"Every Saturday I walked the railroad tracks to pick up laundry and I'd stop by the country store for a Grapette. Sometimes I'd stay at the store awhile, but this day I could see a girl waving to me from the house, telling me to hurry. The girl was ten, two years younger than myself. I ran to see what was wrong.

"Her mother lay on the couch. The couch was covered with a stained blanket. The room did not smell like bread, and the woman's face was gray, her eyes rolling back into her head. She was speaking Polish, and when I asked what she said, the girl told me she was talking about a fire she'd been in many years ago. The girl said her mother had been calling for people they had never heard of, and that her father had gone for the doctor. He wasn't back yet and it had been two hours." Ginny shifted in her chair.

"Her brother stood in the corner of the room playing with a wooden truck. He was about three years old. He wasn't crying, but stood unusually still, only his hands rolling the truck along the wall. The girl said she didn't know what to do, then she said, 'She's dying, isn't she?' And I said I didn't know, but that it looked like it. I asked if her mother recognized her.

"The girl shivered and looked again at her mother's gray face. She motioned for me to sit down. The house was poor but well-kept, and there were clothes draped over the backs of chairs. All the tables were made of dark wood, except the one where they ate: a large block table with thick sturdy legs. I'd never seen one like it and thought maybe they had built it themselves. In the middle of it sat a vase. A few branches of dogwood were stuck in it, and I wondered if the girl had put them there." Lemuel leaned over his knees now and looked straight across the room.

"As I stared at the vase, the Polish woman exhaled once. And there was a slight hum that went along with the air.

The girl jumped as if the sound she heard was thunder. The young boy stopped rolling the truck and went to touch his mother's arm, but the girl pushed him back, nearly knocking him down. I grabbed the boy to keep him from falling and went to get his truck.

"The boy asked, 'Is she asleep?' I said she was. But the girl"—Lemuel turned now to Ginny—"the girl had her ear to her mother's mouth. Listening, I thought, for another hum or message she wanted to hear, because she didn't know what to do and neither did I. So I watched her listening to the open mouth and eyes and hoped when the woman spoke it wouldn't be with those cries she had been making when I walked in, because the girl's ear was so close to her mother's mouth that it would scare her. And I thought she already looked scared and I wanted to comfort her." Ginny nodded.

"In the corner was a wood-burning stove. I went to stoke the ashes and place another stick inside. Then I put water on to boil, because it always seemed a good thing to do at these times. I had seen older people at times of grief turn to the stove and begin to boil or cook food to serve and eat, because it helped lessen the loss somehow. And I knew now that this was death, or I almost knew it. And I didn't want to keep watching the girl with her ear to her mother's open mouth.

"The sound of water boiling made the girl rise and ask what I was doing. I said, 'What would you like?' and she said, 'Coffee,' pulling it down for me from the shelf. I had never before tasted coffee, and probably neither had she, but at the time I figured she drank it every day since she was from a foreign country and maybe did things differently.

"Then she turned to me. She said it was my fault and if I hadn't come her mother wouldn't be dead. She began even to hit me with her fists, yelling and hitting at me. Finally, I told her the coffee was ready and she sat down. The younger boy was crying, though no one comforted him.

"The coffee was almost too dark to drink. We were adding sugar to it when the father came in, saying the doctor was on his way. He looked at his wife on the couch and at the children around the room. Then he gathered us together and held us to him for a long time, even me, squatting down to reach us all. He put his face against our chests, and the girl stood tall, letting it happen. So did the young boy, and so did I. All of us standing taller than the father, but feeling safe in his sturdy arms that reached around us and huddled us to his head.

"The family moved away after that. I didn't know where. But the house on the hill stayed empty, and sometimes I would go to it and see the block table they left there, too heavy to move."

Ginny waited to see what else he would say. She felt the confusion one feels when someone suggests that your ideas of what life should be will fail and that you will not be happy in the ways you thought.

They took Lemuel to the train, saying good-bye and making promises to see each other again. On the way home, the children argued, and light fell on the street as it had years ago. As they rode along, Ginny noticed how the light changed in only a moment's time, and she turned her head to the trees.

The scene was both light and dark. The clouds hung heavy like a ceiling and gave the air an odd gray color above the trees. The road held a brightness that made her squint. When she looked up to see where the light was coming from, she saw no break in the clouds, and when she looked back at the road she thought the light must be coming from somewhere beneath it.

"Don't," Nell whined at her brother.

"Don't." He mocked her and repeated whatever she was doing, which made her scream, "Quit it. Quit."

"Stop that, Jay," Ginny said absently.

Ginny told them to look at the road, at the way the light was falling and how it looked as if it were coming from the ground. They both leaned over the front seat, genuinely interested for a moment.

The wall of trees grew high along the road and made Ginny feel safe. She wanted to keep driving past the turn for her house, past the field two miles away. She wanted to prolong the elation that came as light rose from a place she did not expect, the road shimmering in front of her like a pond or a path she had chosen.

The scene entered her mind as if she were remembering it. And she knew when she thought of this moment years later that nothing would be lost. She was glad she decided to drive home along this road. It was like entering a painting. But when she reached the road that led to her house, she turned in, knowing that such moments could not be prolonged and that trying to prolong them often led to frustration and disappointment, so that the memory would then be tainted. She turned toward home, but tucked the scene inside her, storing it low in her body where it would stay until old age.

"Mom," Jay said. "She tells on everything."

"You poke my ears. I hate that. How would you like to have your ears poked every second?"

He tickled her and she laughed.

Ginny slowed the car and threatened to put them both out on the side of the road and leave them there.

"Put *her* out," said Jay.

A voice came from the floorboard now. "Put *him*."

When Ginny pulled into the driveway, she wondered if it would rain, and what she would fix for dinner. Years ago, when the light had come like this, William had been standing at the stove stirring and tasting dinner with a wooden spoon when she came in. He said what a weird light it was and how he couldn't get over what it had looked like as he came home. She had answered Yes, and kissed him full on the mouth.

The car doors opened and the children scrambled to the kitchen. Ginny could hear "I won" as they hit the refrigerator. When she got out, she heard them running to their rooms. They were laughing. It was so hot that the yard smelled like brass.

She decided to bake bread. As she entered the kitchen, she thought of the Polish home and the man who reached his arms around the tall children. How they stood letting it happen, how he buried his head into their young chests, their warm, lively fragrance like that of blossoms or clover.

Under the Wheat

DOWN IN D-3 I watch the sky gunning through the aperture ninety-odd feet above my head. The missiles are ten months away, and I am lying on my back, listening to the sump. From the bottom of a hole, where the weather is always the same cool sixty-four degrees, plus or minus two, I like to relax and watch the clouds slide through the circle of blue light. I have plenty of time to kill. The aperture is about fifteen feet wide. About the size of a silver dollar from here. A hawk just drifted by. Eagle. Crow. Small cumulus. Nothing. Nothing. Wrapper.

Hot again today, and the sky is drifting across the hole, left to right, a slow thick wind that doesn't gust. When it gusts, it's usually from Canada. Fierce, with hail the size of eyeballs. I've seen wheat go down. Acres and acres of useless straw.

But sometimes it comes out of the southeast, from Bismarck, bringing ten-mile high anvils with it, and you find yourself looking for funnels. This is not tornado country to speak of. The tornado path is to the south and west of here. They walk up from Bismarck and farther south and peter out on the Montana border, rarely touching ground anywhere near this latitude. Still, you keep an eye peeled. I've seen them put down gray fingers to the west, not quite touching but close enough to make you want to find a hole. They say it sounds like freight trains in your yard. I wouldn't know. We are from the coast, where the weather is stable and always predictable because of the ocean. We are trying to adjust.

I make five-hundred a week doing this, driving a company pick up from hole to hole, checking out the sump pumps. I've found only one failure in two months. Twenty feet of black water in the hole and rising. It's the company's biggest headache. The high water table of North Dakota. You can dig twelve feet in any field and have yourself a well. You can dig yourself a shallow hole, come back in a few days and drink. That's why the farmers here have it made. Except for hail. Mostly they are Russians, these farmers.

Karen wants to go back. I have to remind her it's only for one year. Ten more months. Five-hundred a week for a year. But she misses things. The city, her music lessons, movies, the beach, excitement. We live fairly close to a town, but it's one you will never hear of, unless a local goes wild and chainsaws all six members of his family. The movie theater has shown "Bush Pilot," "Red Skies of Montana," "Ice Palace," and "Kon Tiki," so far. These are movies we would not ordinarily pay money to see. She has taken to long walks in the evenings to work out her moods, which are getting harder and harder for me to pretend aren't there. I get time-and-a-half on Saturdays, double-time Sundays and Holidays, and thirteen dollars per diem for the inconvenience of relocating all the way from Oxnard, California. That comes to a lot. You don't walk away from a gold mine like that. I try to tell Karen she has to make the effort, adjust. North Dakota isn't all that bad. As a matter of fact, I sort of enjoy the area. Maybe I am more adaptable. We live close to a large brown lake, an earthfill dam loaded with northern pike. I bought myself a little boat and often go out to troll a bit before the carpool comes by. The freezer is crammed with fish, not one under five pounds.

There's a ghost town on the other side of the lake. The houses were built for the men who worked on the dam. That was years ago. They are paintless now, weeds up to the rotten sills. No glass in the windows, but here and there a rag of drape. Sometimes I take my boat across the lake to the ghost town. I walk the overgrown streets and look into the windows. Sometimes something moves. Rats. Gophers. Wind. Loose boards. Sometimes nothing.

When the weather is out of Canada you can watch it move south, coming like a giant roll of silver dough on the horizon. It gets bigger fast and then you'd better find cover. If the cloud is curdled underneath, you know it means hail. The wind can gust to one-hundred knots. It scares Karen. I tell her there's nothing to worry about. Our trailer is on a good foundation and tied down tight. But she has this dream of being uprooted and of flying away in such a wind. She sees her broken body caught in a tree, magpies picking at it. I tell her the trailer will definitely not budge. Still, she gets wild-eyed and can't light a cigarette.

We're sitting at the dinette table looking out the window, watching the front arrive. You can feel the trailer bucking like a boat at its moorings. Lightning is stroking the blond fields a mile away. To the southeast, I can see a gray finger reaching down. This is unusual, I admit. But I say nothing to Karen. It looks like the two fronts are going to butt heads straight over the trailer park. It's getting dark fast. Something splits the sky behind the trailer and big hail pours out. The streets of the park are white and jumping under the black sky. Karen has her hands up to her ears. There's a stampede on our tin roof. Two TV antennas fold at the same time in a dead faint. A jagged Y of lightning strikes so close you can smell it. Electric steam. Karen is wild, screaming. I can't hear her. Our garbage cans are rising. They are floating past the windows into a flattened wheat field. This is something. Karen's face is closed. She doesn't enjoy it at all, not at all.

I'm tooling around in third on the usual bad road, enjoying the lurches, rolls, and twists. I would not do this to my own truck. The fields I'm driving through are wasted. Head-on with the sky and the sky never loses. I've passed a few unhappy-looking farmers standing in their fields with their hands in their pockets, faces frozen in an expression of disgust, spitting. Toward D-8, just over a rise and down into a narrow gulch, I found a true glacier. It was made out of hail stones welded together by their own impact. It hadn't begun to melt yet. Four feet thick and maybe thirty feet long. You can stand on it and shade your eyes from the white glare. You could tell yourself you are inside the arctic circle. What is this, the return of the Ice Age?

Karen did not cook tonight. Another "mood." I poke around the fridge. I don't know what to say to her anymore. I know it's hard. I can understand that. This is not Oxnard. I'll give her that. I'm the first to admit it. I pop a beer and sit down at the table opposite her. Our eyes don't meet. They haven't for weeks. We are like two magnetic north poles, repelling each other for invisible reasons. Last night in bed I touched her. She went stiff. She didn't have to say a word. I took my hand back. I got the message. There was the hum

of the air-conditioner and nothing else. The world could
have been filled with dead bodies. I turned on the lights. She
got up and lit a cigarette after two tries. Nerves. "I'm going
for a walk, Lloyd," she said, checking the sky. "Maybe we
should have a baby?" I said. "I'm making plenty of money."
But she looked at me as if I had picked up an ax.

I would like to know where she finds to go and what she
finds to do there. She hates the town worse than the trailer
park. The trailer park has a rec hall and a social club for the
wives. But she won't take advantage of that. I know the
neighbors are talking. They think she's a snob. They think I
spoil her. After she left I went out on the porch and drank
eleven beers. Let them talk.

Three farm kids. Just standing outside the locked gate of
D-4. "What do you kids want?" I know what they want. A
"look-see." Security measures are in effect, but what the
hell. There is nothing here yet but a ninety-foot hole with a
tarp on it and a sump pump in the bottom. They are excited. They want to know what ICBM stands for. What is a
warhead? How fast is it? How do you know if it's really
going to smear the right town? What if it went straight up
and came straight down? Can you hit the moon? "Look at
the sky up there, kids," I tell them. "Lie on your backs, like
this, and after a while you sort of get the feeling you're
looking *down,* from on top of it." The kids lie down on the
concrete. Kids have a way of giving all their attention to
something interesting. I swear them to secrecy, not for my
protection, because who cares, but because it will make
their day. They will run home, busting with secret info. I
drive off to D-9, where the sump trouble was.

Caught three lunkers this morning. All over twenty-four inches. It's seven a.m. now and I'm on Ruby Street, the ghost town. The streets are all named after stones. Why I don't know. This is nothing like anything we have on the coast. Karen doesn't like the climate or the people and the flat sky presses down on her from all sides and gives her bad dreams, sleeping and awake. But what can I *do*?

I'm on Onyx Street, number 49, a two-bedroom bungalow with a few pieces of furniture left in it. There is a chest of drawers in the bedroom, a bed with a rotten gray mattress. There is a closet with a raggedy slip in it. The slip has brown water stains on it. In the bottom of the chest is a magazine, yellow with age. *Secret Confessions*. I can imagine the woman who lived here with her husband. Not much like Karen at all. But what did she do while her husband was off working on the dam? Did she stand at this window in her slip and wish she were back in Oxnard? Did she cry her eyes out on this bed and think crazy thoughts? Where is she now? Does she think, "This is July 15, 1962, and I am glad I am not in North Dakota anymore"? Did she take long walks at night and not cook? I have an impulse to do something odd, and do it.

When a thunderhead passes over a cyclone fence that surrounds a site, such as the one passing over D-6 now, you can hear the wire hiss with nervous electrons. It scares me because the fence is a perfect lightning rod, a good conductor. But I stay on my toes. Sometimes, when a big cumulus is overhead stroking the area and roaring, I'll just stay put in my truck until it's had its fun.

Because this is Sunday, I am making better than twelve dollars an hour. I'm driving through a small farming community called Spacebow. A Russian word, I think, be-

cause you're supposed to pronounce the *e*. No one I know
does. Shade trees on every street. A Russian church here,
grain elevator there. No wind. Hot for nine a.m. Men
dressed in Sunday black. Ladies in their best. Kids looking
uncomfortable and controlled. Even the dogs are behaving.
There is a woman, manless I think, because I've seen her before, always alone on her porch, eyes on something far
away. A "thinker." Before today I've only waved hello.
First one finger off the wheel, nod, then around the block
once again and the whole hand out the window and a smile.
That was last week. After the first turn past her place today
she waves back. A weak hand at first, as if she's not sure
that's what I meant. But after a few times around the block
she knows that's what I meant. And so I'm stopping. I'm
going to ask for a cup of cold water. I'm thirsty anyway.
Maybe all this sounds hokey to you if you are from some big
town like Oxnard, but this is not a big town like Oxnard.

Her name is Myrna Dan. That last name must be a
pruned-down version of Danielovitch or something because
the people here are mostly Russians. She is thirty-two, a
widow, one brat. A two-year old named "Piper," crusty
with food. She owns a small farm here but there is no one to
work it. She has a decent allotment from the U.S. Govern-
ment and a vegetable garden. If you are from the coast you
would not stop what you were doing to look at her. Her
hands are square and the fingers stubby, made for rough
wooden handles. Hips like gateposts.

No supper again. Karen left a note. "Lloyd, I am going
for a walk. There are some cold cuts in the fridge." It wasn't
even signed. Just like that. One of these days on one of her
walks she is going to get caught by the sky which can change
on you in a minute.

Bill Finkel made a remark on the way in to the dispatch center. It was a little personal and coming from anybody else I would have called him on it. But he is the lead engineer, the boss. A few of the other guys grinned behind their hands. How do I know where she goes or why? I am not a swami. If it settles her nerves, why should I push it? I've thought of sending her to Ventura to live with her mother for a while, but her mother is getting senile and has taken to writing mean letters. I tell Karen the old lady is around the bend, don't take those letters too seriously. But what's the use when the letters come in like clockwork, once a week, page after page of nasty accusations in a big, inch-high scrawl, like a kid's, naming things that never happened. Karen takes it hard, no matter what I say, as if what the old lady says is true.

Spacebow looks deserted. It isn't. The men are off in the fields, the women are inside working toward evening. Too hot outside even for the dogs who are sleeping under the porches. Ninety-nine. I stopped for water at Myrna's. Do you want to see a missile silo? Sure, she said, goddamn rights, just like that. I have an extra hard hat in the truck but she doesn't have to wear it if she doesn't want to. Regulations at this stage of the program are a little pointless. Just a hole with a sump in it. Of course you can fall into it and get yourself killed. That's about the only danger. But there are no regulations that can save you from your own stupidity. Last winter when these holes were being dug, a kid walked out on a tarp. The tarp was covered with light snow and he couldn't tell where the ground ended and the hole began. He dropped the whole ninety feet and his hardhat did not save his ass. Myrna is impressed with this story. She is very anxious to see one. D-7 is closest to Spacebow, only a mile out of town. It isn't on my schedule today, but so what. I hand her the orange hat. She has trouble with the chin strap. I help her cinch it. Piper wants to wear it too and grabs at the straps, whining. Myrna has big jaws. Strong. But not in an ugly way.

I tell her the story about Jack Stern, the Jewish quality control man from St. Louis who took flying lessons because he wanted to be able to get to a decent size city in a hurry whenever he felt the need. This flat empty farm land made his ulcer flare. He didn't know how to drive a car, and yet there he was, tearing around the sky in a Bonanza. One day he flew into a giant hammerhead—thinking, I guess, that a cloud like that is nothing but a lot of water vapor, no matter what shape it has or how big—and was never heard from again. That cloud ate him and the Bonanza. At the airport up in Minot they picked up two words on the emergency frequency, *Oh no,* then static.

I tell her the story about the motor-pool secretary who shot her husband once in the neck and twice in the foot with a target pistol while he slept. Both of them pulling down good money, too. I tell her the one about the one that got away. A northern as big as a shark. Pulled me and my boat a mile before my twelve-pound test monofilament snapped. She gives me a sidelong glance and makes a buzzing sound as if to say, *That* one takes the cake, Mister! We are on the bottom of D-10, watching the circle of sky, lying on our backs.

The trailer *stinks.* I could smell it from the street as soon as I got out of Bill Finkel's car. Fish heads. *Heads!* I guess they've been sitting there like that most of the afternoon. Just the big alligator jaws of my big beautiful pikes, but not the bodies. A platter of them, uncooked, drying out, and getting high. Knife fork napkin glass. I'd like to know what goes on inside her head, what passes for thinking in there. The note: "Lloyd, Eat your fill." Not signed. Is this supposed to be humor? I fail to get the point of it. I have to carry the mess to the garbage cans without breathing. A wind has come up. From the southeast. A big white fire is blazing in the sky over my shoulder. You can hear the far-off rumble, like a whale grunting. I squint west, checking for funnels.

Trouble in D-7. Busted sump. I pick up Myrna and Piper and head for the hole. It's a nice day for a drive. It could be a bearing seizure, but that's only a percentage guess. I unlock the gate and we drive to the edge of it. Space age artillery, I explain, as we stand on the lip of D-7, feeling the vertigo. The tarp is off for maintenance and the hole is solid black. If you let your imagination run, you might see it as bottomless. The "Pit" itself. Myrna is holding Piper back. Piper is whining, she wants to see the hole. Myrna has to slap her away, scolding. I drain my beer and let the can drop. I don't hear it hit. Not even a splash. I grab the fussing kid and hold her out over the hole. "Have yourself a *good* look, brat," I say. I hold her by the ankle with one hand. She is paralyzed. Myrna goes so white I have to smile. "Oh wait," she says. "Please, Lloyd. No." As if I ever would.

Myrna wants to see the D-flight control center. I ask her if she has claustrophobia. She laughs, but it's no joke. That far below the surface inside that capsule behind an eight-ton door can be upsetting if you're susceptible to confinement. The elevator is slow and heavy, designed to haul equipment. The door opens on a dimly-lit room. Spooky. There's crated gear scattered around. And there is the door, one yard thick to withstand the shock waves from the Bomb. I wheel it open. Piper whines, her big eyes distrustful. There is a musty smell in the dank air. The lights and blower are on now, but it will take a while for the air to freshen itself up. I wheel the big door shut. It can't latch yet, but Myrna is impressed. I explain to her what goes on in here. We sit down at the console. I show her where the launch "enabling" switches will be and why it will take two people together to launch an attack, the chairs fifteen feet apart and both switches turned for a several second count before the firing sequence can start, in case one guy goes berserk and decides to end the world because his old lady has been holding out on him, or just for the hell of it, given human nature. I show her the escape hole. It's loaded with ordinary sand. You pull this chain and the sand dumps into the capsule. Then you climb up the tube that held the sand into someone's wheat field. I show her the toilet and the little kitchen. I can see there is something on her mind. Isolated places make you think of weird things. It's happened to me more than once. Not here, but in the ghost town on the other side of the lake.

Topside the weather has changed. The sky is the color of pikebelly, wind rising from the southeast. To the west I can see stubby funnels pushing down from the overcast, but only so far. It looks like the clouds are growing roots. We have to run back to the truck in the rain, Piper screaming on Myrna's hip. A heavy bolt strikes less than a mile away. A blue fireball sizzles where it hits. Smell the ozone. It makes me sneeze.

This is the second day she's been gone. I don't know where or how. All her clothes are here. She doesn't have any money. I don't know what to do. There is no police station. Do I call her mother? Do I notify the FBI? The highway patrol? Bill Finkel?

Everybody in the carpool knows but won't say a word, out of respect for my feelings. Bill Finkel has other things on his mind. He is worried about rumored economy measures in the Assembly and Check-Out program next year. It has nothing to do with me. My job ends before the phase begins. I guess she went back to Oxnard, or maybe Ventura. But how?

We are in the D-flight control center. Myrna, with her hardhat cocked to one side, wants to fool around with the incomplete equipment. Piper is with her grandma. We are seated at the control console and she is pretending to work her switch. She has me pretend to work my switch. She wants to launch the entire flight of missiles, D-1 through D-10, at Cuba or Panama. Why Cuba and Panama? I ask. What about Russia? Why not Cuba or Panama? she says. Besides, I have Russian blood. Everyone around here has Russian blood. No, it's Cuba and Panama. Just think of the looks on their faces. All those people lying in the sun on the decks of those big white holiday boats, the coolies out in the cane fields, the tin horn generals, and the whole shiteree. They'll look up trying to shade their eyes but they won't be able to. What in hell is this all about, they'll say, then *zap,* poof, *gone.*

I feel it too, craziness like hers. What if I couldn't get that eight-ton door open, Myrna? I see her hardhat wobble, her lip drop. What if? Just what *if?* She puts her arms around me and our hardhats click. She is one strong woman.

Lloyd, Lloyd, she says.

Yo, I say.

Jesus. *Jesus.*

Easy, easy.

Lloyd!

Bingo.

It's good down here — no *rules* — and she goes berserk. But later she is calm and up to mischief again. I recognize the look now. Okay, I tell her. What *next,* Myrna? She wants to do something halfway nasty. This, believe me, doesn't surprise me at all.

I'm sitting on the steel floor listening to the blower and waiting for Myrna to finish her business. I'm trying hard to picture what the weather is doing topside. It's not easy to do. It could be clear and calm and blue or it could be wild. There could be a high thin overcast or there could be nothing. You just can't know when you're this far under the wheat. I can hear her trying to work the little chrome lever, even though I told her there's no plumbing yet. Some maintenance yokel is going to find Myrna's "surprise." She comes out, pretending to be sheepish, but I can see that the little joke tickles her.

Something takes my hook and strips off ten yards of line then stops dead. Snag. I reel in. The pole is bent double and the line is singing. Then something lets go but it isn't the line because I'm still snagged. It breaks the surface, a lady's shoe. It's brown and white with a short heel. I toss it into the bottom of the boat. The water is shallow here, and clear. There's something dark and wide under me like a shadow on the water. An old farmhouse, submerged when the dam filled. There's a deep current around the structure. I can see fence, tires, an old truck, feed pens. There is a fat farmer in the yard staring up at me, checking the weather, and I jump away from him, almost tipping the boat. My heart feels tangled in my ribs. But it's only a stump with arms.

The current takes my boat in easy circles. A swimmer would be in serious trouble. I crank up the engine and head back. No fish today. So be it. Sometimes you come home empty-handed. The shoe is new, stylish, and was made in Spain.

I'm standing on the buckled porch of 49 Onyx Street. Myrna is inside reading *Secret Confessions:* "What My Don Must Never Know." The sky is bad. The lake is bad. It will be a while before we can cross back. I knock on the door, as we planned. Myrna is on the bed in the stained, raggedy slip, giggling. "Listen to this dogshit, Lloyd," she says. But I'm not in the mood for weird stories. "I brought you something, honey," I say. She looks at the soggy shoe. "That?" But she agrees to try it on, anyway. I feel like my own ghost, bumping into the familiar but run-down walls of my old house in the middle of nowhere, and I remember my hatred of it. "Hurry up," I say, my voice true as a razor.

A thick tube hairy with rain is snaking out of the sky less than a mile away. Is it going to touch? "They never do, Lloyd. This isn't Kansas. Will you please listen to this dogshit?" Something about a pregnant high school girl, Dee, locked in a toilet with a knitting needle. Something about this Don who believes in purity. Something about bright red blood. Something about ministers and mothers and old-fashioned shame. I'm not listening, even when Dee slides the big needle in. I have to keep watch on the sky, because there is a first time for everything, even if this is not Kansas. The wind is stripping shingles from every roof I see. A long board is spinning like a slow propeller. The funnel is behind a bluff, holding back. But I can hear it, the freight trains. Myrna is standing behind me, running a knuckle up and down my back. "Hi, darling," she says. "Want to know what I did while you were out working on the dam today?" The dark tube has begun to move out from behind the bluff, but I'm not sure which way. "Tell me," I say. "Tell me."

Simmering

IT STARTED in the backyards. At first the men concentrated on heat and smoke, and on dangerous thrusts with long forks. Their wives gave them aprons in railroad stripes, with slogans on the front— *Hot Stuff, The Boss* — to spur them on. Then it began to get all mixed up with who should do the dishes, and you can't fall back on paper plates forever, and around that time the wives got tired of making butterscotch brownies and jello salads with grated carrots and baby marshmallows in them and wanted to make money instead, and one thing led to another. The wives said that there were only twenty-four hours in a day; and the men, who in that century were still priding themselves on their rationality, had to agree that this was so.

For a while they worked it out that the men were in charge of the more masculine kinds of food: roasts, chops, steaks, dead chickens and ducks, gizzards, hearts, anything that had obviously been killed, that had visibly bled. The wives did the other things, the glazed parsnips and the prune whip, anything that flowered or fruited or was soft and gooey in the middle. That was all right for about a decade. Everyone praised the men to keep them going, and the wives, sneaking out of the houses in the mornings with their squeaky new briefcases, clutching their bus tickets because the men needed the station wagons to bring home the carcasses, felt they had got away with something.

But time is not static, and the men refused to stay put. They could not be kept isolated in their individual kitchens, kitchens into which the wives were allowed less and less frequently because, the men said, they did not sharpen the knives properly, if at all. The men began to acquire kitchen machines, which they would spend the weekends taking apart and oiling. There were a few accidents at first, a few lost fingers and ends of noses, but the men soon got the hang of it and branched out into other areas: automatic nutmeg graters, electric gadgets for taking the lids off jars. At cocktail parties they would gather in groups at one end of the room, exchanging private recipes and cooking yarns, tales of soufflés daringly saved at the last minute, pears flambées which had gone out of control and had to be fought to a standstill. Some of these stories had risqué phrases in them, such as *chicken breasts*. Indeed, sexual metaphor was changing: bowls and forks became prominent, and *eggbeater, pressure cooker* and *turkey baster* became words which only the most daring young women, the kind who thought it was a kick to butter their own toast, would venture to pronounce in mixed company. Men who could not cook very well hung about the edges of these groups, afraid to say much, admiring the older and more experienced ones, wishing they could be like them.

Soon after that, the men resigned from their jobs in large numbers so they could spend more time in the kitchen. The magazines said it was a modern trend. The wives were all driven off to work, whether they wanted to or not: someone had to make the money, and of course they did not want their husbands' masculinity to be threatened. A man's status in the community was now displayed by the length of his carving knives, by how many of them he had and how sharp he kept them, and by whether they were plain or ornamented with gold and precious jewels.

Exclusive clubs and secret societies sprang up. Men meeting for the first time would now exchange special handshakes—the Béchamel twist, the chocolate mousse double grip—to show that they had been initiated. It was pointed out to the women, who by this time did not go into the kitchens at all on pain of being thought unfeminine, that *chef* after all means *chief* and that Mixmasters were common but no one had ever heard of a Mixmistress. Psychological articles began to appear in the magazines on the origin of women's kitchen envy and how it could be cured. Amputation of the tip of the tongue was recommended, and, as you know, became a widespread practice in the more advanced nations. If Nature had meant women to cook, it was said, God would have made carving knives round and with holes in them.

This is history. But it is not a history familiar to many people. It exists only in the few archival collections that have not yet been destroyed, and in manuscripts like this one, passed from woman to woman, usually at night, copied out by hand or memorized. It is subversive of me even to write these words. I am doing so, at the risk of my own personal freedom, because now, after so many centuries of stagnation, there are signs that hope and therefore change have once more become possible.

The women in their pinstripe suits, exiled to the livingrooms where they dutifully sip the glasses of port brought out to them by the men, used to sit uneasily, silently, listening to the loud bursts of male and somehow derisive laughter from behind the closed kitchen doors. But they have begun whispering to each other. When they are with those they trust, they tell of a time long ago, lost in the fogs of legend, hinted at in packets of letters found in attic trunks and in the cryptic frescoes on abandoned temple walls, when women too were allowed to participate in the ritual which now embodies the deepest religious convictions of our society: the transformation of the consecrated flour into the holy bread. At night they dream, long clandestine dreams, confused and obscured by shadows. They dream of plunging their hands into the earth, which is red as blood and soft, which is milky and warm. They dream that the earth gathers itself under their hands, swells, changes in form, flowers into a thousand shapes, for them too, for them once more. They dream of apples; they dream of the creation of the world; they dream of freedom.

Our Story Begins

THE FOG blew in early again. This was the tenth straight day of it. The waiters and waitresses gathered along the window to watch, and Charlie pushed his cart across the dining room so that he could watch with them as he filled the water glasses. Boats were beating in ahead of the fog, which loomed behind them like a tall rolling breaker. Gulls glided from the sky to the pylons along the wharf, where they shook out their feathers and rocked from side to side and glared at the tourists passing by.

The fog covered the stanchions of the bridge. The bridge appeared to be floating upon the fog, which billowed into the harbor and began to overtake the boats. One by one they were swallowed up in it.

"Now that's what I call hairy," one of the waiters said. "You couldn't get me out there for love or money."

A waitress said something and the rest of them laughed.

"Nice talk," the waiter said.

The maître d' came out of the kitchen and snapped his fingers. "Busboy!" he called. One of the waitresses turned and looked at Charlie, who put down the pitcher he was pouring from and pushed his cart back across the dining room to its assigned place. For the next half hour, until the first customer came in, Charlie folded napkins and laid out squares of butter in little bowls filled with crushed ice, and thought of the things he would do to the maître d' if he ever got the maître d' in his power.

But this was a diversion; he didn't really hate the maître d'. He hated his meaningless work and his fear of being fired from it, and most of all he hated being called a busboy, because being called a busboy made it harder for him to think of himself as a man, which he was just learning to do.

Only a few tourists came into the restaurant that night. All of them were alone, and plainly disappointed. They sat by themselves, across from their shopping bags, and stared morosely in the direction of the Golden Gate though there was nothing to see but the fog pressing up against the windows and greasy drops of water running down the glass. Like most people who ate alone they ordered the bargain items, scampi or cod or the Capn's Plate, and maybe a small carafe of the house wine. The waiters neglected them. The tourists dawdled over their food, overtipped the waiters, and left more deeply sunk in disappointment than before.

At nine o'clock the maître d' sent all but three of the waiters home, then went home himself. Charlie hoped he'd be given the nod too, but he was left standing by his cart, where he folded more napkins and replaced the ice as it melted in the water glasses and under the squares of butter. The three waiters kept going back to the storeroom to smoke dope. By the time the restaurant closed they were so wrecked they could hardly stand.

Charlie started home the long way, up Columbus Avenue, because Columbus Avenue had the brightest streetlights. But in this fog the lights were only a presence, a milky blotch here and there in the vapor above. Charlie walked slowly and kept to the walls. He met no one on his way; but once, as he paused to wipe the dampness from his face, he heard strange ticking steps behind him and turned to see a three-legged dog appear out of the mist. It moved past in a series of lurches and was gone. "Jesus," Charlie said. Then he laughed to himself, but the sound was unconvincing and he decided to get off the street for a while.

Just around the corner on Vallejo there was a coffeehouse where Charlie sometimes went on his nights off. Jack Kerouac had mentioned this particular coffee shop in *The Subterraneans*. These days the patrons were mostly Italian people who came to listen to the jukebox, which was filled with music from Italian operas, but Charlie always looked up when someone came in the door; it might be Ginsberg or Corso, stopping by for old times' sake. He liked sitting there with an open book on the table listening to music that he thought of as being classical. He liked to imagine that the rude, sluggish woman who brought him his cappuccino had once been Neal Cassady's lover. It was possible.

When Charlie came into the coffeehouse the only other customers were four old men sitting by the door. He took a table across the room. Someone had left an Italian movie magazine on the chair next to his. Charlie looked through the photographs, keeping time with his fingers to "The Anvil Chorus" while the waitress made up his cappuccino. The coffee machine hissed as he worked the handle. The room filled with the sweet smell of coffee. Charlie also caught the smell of fish and realized that it came from him, that he was reeking of it. His fingers fell still on the table.

Charlie paid the waitress when she served him. He intended to drink up and get out. While he was waiting for the coffee to cool, a woman came in the door with two men. They looked around, held a conference, and finally sat down at the table next to Charlie's. As soon as they were seated they began to talk without regard for whether Charlie could hear them. He listened, and after a time he began to glance over at them. Either they didn't notice or they didn't care. They were indifferent to his presence.

Charlie gathered from their conversation that they were members of a church choir, making the rounds after choir practice. The woman's name was Audrey. Her lipstick was smeared, making her mouth look a little crooked. She had a gaunt face with thick black brows that she raised skeptically whenever her husband spoke. Audrey's husband was tall and heavy. He shifted constantly, scraping his chair as he did so, and moved his hat back and forth from one knee to the other. Big as he was, the green suit he wore fit him perfectly. His name was Truman, and the other man's name was George. George had a calm, reedy voice that he enjoyed using; Charlie could see him listening to it as he talked. He was a teacher of some kind, which did not surprise Charlie. George looked at him like the young professors he'd had during his three years of college: rimless spectacles, turtle-neck sweater, the ghost of a smile always on his lips. But George wasn't really young. His thick hair, parted in the middle, had begun to turn gray.

No—it seemed that only Audrey and George sang in the choir. They were telling Truman about a trip the choir had just made to Los Angeles, to a festival of choirs. Truman looked from his wife to George as each of them spoke, and shook his head as they described the sorry characters of the other members of the choir, and the eccentricities of the choir director.

"Of course Father Wes is nothing compared to Monsignor Strauss," George said. "Monsignor Strauss was positively certifiable."

"Strauss?" Truman said. "Which one is Strauss? The only Strauss I know is Johann." Truman looked at his wife and laughed.

"Forgive me," George said. "I was being cryptic. George sometimes forgets the basics. When you've met someone like Monsignor Strauss, you naturally assume that everyone else has heard of him. The Monsignor was our director for five years, prior to Father Wes's tenure. He got religion and left for the subcontinent just before Audrey joined us, so of course you wouldn't recognize the name."

"The subcontinent," Truman said. "What's that? Atlantis?" He laughed again.

"For God's sake, Truman," Audrey said. "Sometimes you embarrass me."

"India," George said. "Calcutta. Mother Teresa and all that."

Audrey put her hand on George's arm. "George," she said, "tell Truman that marvelous story you told me about Monsignor Strauss and the Filipino."

George smiled to himself. "Ah yes," he said. "Miguel. That's a long story, Audrey. Perhaps another night would be better."

"Oh no," said Audrey. "Tonight would be perfect."

Truman said, "If it's that long..."

"It's not," Audrey said. She knocked on the table with her knuckles. "Tell the story, George."

George looked over at Truman and shrugged. "Don't blame George," he said. He drank off the last of his brandy. "All right then. Our story begins. Monsignor Strauss had some money from somewhere, and every year he made a journey to points exotic. When he came home he always had some unusual souvenir that he'd picked up on his travels. From Argentina he brought everyone seeds which grew into plants whose flowers smelled like, excuse me, *merde.* He got them in an Argentine joke shop, if you can imagine such a thing. When he came back from Kenya he smuggled in a lizard that could pick off flies with its tongue from a distance of six feet. The Monsignor carried this lizard around on his finger and whenever a fly came within range he would say 'Watch this!' and aim the lizard like a pistol, and *poof*—no more fly."

Audrey pointed her finger at Truman and said, "Poof." Truman just looked at her. "I need another drink," Audrey said, and signaled the waitress.

George ran his finger around the rim of his snifter. "After the lizard," he said, "there was a large Australian rodent that ended up in the zoo, and after the rodent came a nineteen-year-old human being from the Philippines. His name was Miguel Lopez de Constanza, and he was a cabdriver from Manila the Monsignor had hired as a chauffeur during his stay there and taken a liking to. When the Monsignor got back he pulled some strings at Immigration and a few weeks later Miguel showed up. He spoke no English, really —only a few buzz words for tourists in Manila. The first month or so he stayed with Monsignor Strauss in the rectory, then he found a room in the Hotel Overland and moved in there."

"The Hotel Overland," Truman said. "That's that druggy hangout on upper Grant."

"The Hotel Overdose," Audrey said. When Truman looked at her she said, "That's what they call it."

"You seem to be up on all the nomenclature," Truman said.

The waitress came with their drinks. When her tray was empty she stood behind Truman and began to write in a notebook she carried. Charlie hoped she wouldn't come over to his table. He did not want the others to notice him. They would guess that he'd been listening to them, and they might not like it. They might stop talking. But the waitress finished making her entries and moved back to the bar without a glance at Charlie.

The old men by the door were arguing in Italian. The window above them was all steamed up, and Charlie could feel the closeness of the fog outside. The jukebox glowed in the corner. The song that was playing ended abruptly, the machinery whirred, and "The Anvil Chorus" came on again.

"So why the Hotel Overland?" Truman asked.

"Truman prefers the Fairmont," Audrey said. "Truman thinks everyone should stay at the Fairmont."

"Miguel had no money," George said. "Only what the Monsignor gave him. The idea was that he would stay there long enough to learn English and pick up a trade. Then he could get a job. Take care of himself."

"Sounds reasonable," Truman said.

Audrey laughed. "Truman, you slay me. That is *exactly* what I thought you would say. Now let's just turn things around for a minute. Let's say that for some reason you, Truman, find yourself in Manila dead broke. You don't know anybody, you don't understand anything anyone says, and you wind up in a hotel where people are sticking needles into themselves and nodding out on the stairs and setting their rooms on fire all the time. How much Spanish are you going to learn living like that? What kind of trade are you going to pick up? Get real," Audrey said. "That's not a reasonable existence."

"San Francisco isn't Manila," Truman said. "Believe me—I've been there. At least here you've got a chance. And it isn't true that he didn't know anybody. What about the Monsignor?"

"Terrific," Audrey said. "A priest who walks around with a lizard on his finger. Great friend. Or, as you would say, great connection."

"I have never, to my knowledge, used the word *connection* in that way," Truman said.

George had been staring into his brandy snifter, which he held cupped in both hands. He looked up at Audrey. "Actually," he said, "Miguel was not entirely at a loss. In fact, he managed pretty well for a time. Monsignor Strauss got him into a training course for mechanics at the Porsche-Audi place on Van Ness, and he picked up English at a terrific rate. It's amazing, isn't it, what one can do if one has no choice." George rolled the snifter back and forth between his palms. "The druggies left him completely alone, incredible as that may seem. No hassles in the hallways, nothing. It was as if Miguel lived in a different dimension from them, and in a way he did. He went to Mass every day, and sang in the choir. That's where I made his acquaintance. Miguel had a gorgeous baritone, truly gorgeous. He was extremely proud of his voice. He was proud of his body, too. Ate precisely so much of this, so much of that. Did elaborate exercises every day. He even gave himself facial massages to keep from getting a double chin."

"There you are," Truman said to Audrey. "There is such a thing as character." When she didn't answer he added, "What I'm getting at is that people are not necessarily limited by their circumstances."

I know what you're getting at," Audrey said. "The story isn't over yet."

Truman moved his hat from his knee to the table. He folded his arms across his chest. "I've got a full day ahead of me," he said to Audrey. She nodded but did not look at him.

George took a sip of his brandy. He closed his eyes afterward and ran the tip of his tongue around his lips. Then he lowered his head again and stared back into the snifter. "Miguel met a woman," he said, "as do we all. Her name was Senga. My guess is that she had originally been called Agnes, and that she turned her name around in hopes of making herself more interesting to people of the male persuasion. Senga was older than Miguel by at least ten years, maybe more. She had a daughter in, I believe, fifth grade. Senga was a finance officer at B of A. I don't remember how they met. They went out for a while, then Senga broke it off. I suppose it was a casual thing for her, but for Miguel it was serious. He worshipped Senga, and I use that word advisedly. He set up a little shrine to her in his room. A high school graduation picture of Senga surrounded by different objects that she had worn or used. Combs. Handkerchiefs. Empty perfume bottles. A whole pile of things. How he got them I have no idea—whether she gave them to him or whether he just took them. The odd thing is, he only went out with her a few times. I very much doubt that they ever reached the point of sleeping together."

"They didn't," Truman said.

George looked up at him.

"If he'd slept with her," Truman said, "he wouldn't have built a shrine to her."

Audrey shook her head. "Pure Truman," she said. "Vintage Truman."

He patted her arm. "No offense," he told her.

"Be that as it may," George said, "Miguel wouldn't give up, and that's what caused all the trouble. First he wrote her letters, long mushy letters in broken English. He gave me one to read through for spelling and so on, but it was utterly hopeless. All fragments and run-ons. No paragraphs. I just gave it back after a few days and said it was fine. Miguel thought that the letters would bring Senga around, but she never answered and after a while he began calling her at all hours. She wouldn't talk to him. As soon as she heard his voice she hung up. Eventually she got an unlisted number. She wouldn't talk to Miguel, but Miguel thought that she would listen to yours truly. He wanted me to go down to B of A and plead his cause. Act as a kind of character witness. Which, after some reflection, I agreed to do."

"Oho," Truman said. "The plot thickens. Enter Miles Standish."

"I *knew* you'd say that," Audrey said. She finished her drink and looked around, but the waitress was sitting at the bar with her back to the room, smoking a cigarette.

George took his glasses off, held them up to the light, and put them on again. He smiled down at the table. "So," he said, "George sallies forth to meet Senga. Senga—doesn't it make you think of a jungle queen, that name? Flashing eyes, dagger at the hip, breasts bulging over a leopard-skin halter? Such was not the case. This Senga was still an Agnes. Thin. Businesslike. And *very* grouchy. No sooner did I mention Miguel's name than I was shown the door, with a message for Miguel: if he bothered her again she would set the police on him.

"'Set the police on him.' Those were her words, and she meant them. A week or so later Miguel followed her home from work and she forthwith got a lawyer on the case. The upshot of it was that Miguel had to sign a paper saying that he understood he would be arrested if he wrote, called, or followed Senga again. He signed, but with his fingers crossed, as it were. He told me, 'Horhay, I sign—but I do not accept.' 'Nobly spoken,' I told him, 'but you'd damn well better accept or that woman will have you locked up.' Miguel said that prison did not frighten him, that in his country all the best people were in prison. Sure enough, a few days later he followed Senga home again and she did it—she had him locked up."

"Poor kid," Audrey said.

Truman had been trying to get the attention of the waitress, who wouldn't look at him. He turned to Audrey. "What do you mean, 'Poor kid'? What about the girl? Senga? She's trying to hold down a job and feed her daughter and meanwhile she has this Filipino stalking her all over the city. If you want to feel sorry for someone feel sorry for her."

"I do," Audrey said.

"All right then." Truman looked back toward the waitress again, and as he did so Audrey picked up George's snifter and took a drink from it. George smiled at her. "What's wrong with that woman?" Truman said. He shook his head. "I give up."

"George, go on," Audrey said.

George nodded. "In brief," he said, "it was a serious mess. *Très sérieux.* They set bail at twenty thousand dollars, which Monsignor Strauss could not raise. Nor, it goes without saying, could yours truly. So Miguel remained in jail. Senga's lawyer was out for blood, and he got Immigration into the act. They were threatening to revoke Miguel's visa and throw him out of the country. Monsignor Strauss finally got him off, but it was, as the Duke said, a damn close-run thing. It turned out that Senga was going to be transferred to Portland in a month or so, and the Monsignor persuaded her to drop charges with the understanding that Miguel would not come within ten miles of the city limits as long as she lived there. Until she left, Miguel would stay with Monsignor Strauss at the rectory, under his personal supervision. The Monsignor also agreed to pay Senga for her lawyer's fees, which were outrageous. Absolutely outrageous."

"So what was the bottom line?" Truman asked.

"Simplicity itself," George said. "If Miguel messed up they'd throw him on the first plane to Manila."

"Sounds illegal," Truman said.

"Perhaps. But that was the arrangement."

A new song began on the jukebox. The men by the door stopped arguing, and each of them seemed all at once to draw into himself.

"Listen," Audrey said. "It's him. Caruso."

The record was worn and gave the effect of static behind Caruso's voice. The music coming through the static made Charlie think of the cultural broadcasts from Europe his parents listened to so solemnly when he was a boy. At times Caruso's voice was almost lost, and then it would surge again. The old men were still. One of them began to weep. The tears fell freely from his open eyes, down his shining cheeks.

"So that was Caruso," Truman said when it ended. "I always wondered what all the fuss was about. Now I know. That's what I call singing." Truman took out his wallet and put some money on the table. He examined the money left in the wallet before putting it away. "Ready?" he said to Audrey.

"No," Audrey said. "Finish the story, George."

George took his glasses off and laid them next to the snifter. He rubbed his eyes. "All right," he said. "Back to Miguel. As per the agreement, he lived in the rectory until Senga moved to Portland. Behaved himself, too. No letters, no calls, no following her around. In his pajamas every night by ten. Then Senga left town and Miguel went back to his room at the Overland. For a while there he looked pretty desperate, but after a few weeks he seemed to come out of it.

"I say 'seemed.' There was in fact more going on than met the eye. My eye, anyway. One night I am sitting at home and listening, believe it or not, to *Tristan,* when the telephone rings. At first no one says anything, then this voice comes on the line whispering, 'Help me, Horhay, help me,' and of course I know who it is. He says he needs to see me right away. No explanation. He doesn't even tell me where he is. I just have to assume that he's at the Overland and that's where I find him, in the lobby."

George gave a little laugh. "Actually," he said, "I almost missed him. His face was all bandaged up, from his nose to the top of his forehead. If I hadn't been looking for him I never would have recognized him. Never. He was sitting there with his suitcases all around him and a white cane across his knees. When I made my presence known to him he said, 'Horhay, I am blind.' How, I asked him, had this come to pass? He would not say. Instead he gave me a piece of paper with a telephone number on it and asked me to call Senga and tell her that he had gone blind, and that he would be arriving in Portland by Trailways at eleven o'clock the next morning."

"Great Scott," Truman said. "He was faking it, wasn't he? I mean, he wasn't really blind, was he?"

"Now that is an interesting question," George said. "Because while I would have to say that Miguel was not really blind, I would also have to say that he was not really faking it, either. But to go on. Senga was unmoved. She instructed me to tell Miguel that not she but the police would be waiting to meet his bus. Miguel didn't believe her. 'Horhay,' he said, 'she will be there,' and that was that. End of discussion."

"Did he go?" Truman asked.

"Of course he went," Audrey said. "He loved her."

George nodded. "I put him on the bus myself. Led him to his seat, in fact."

"So he still had the bandages on," Truman said.

"Oh yes. Yes, he still had them on."

"But that's a twelve, thirteen-hour ride. If there wasn't anything wrong with his eyes, why didn't he just take the bandages off and put them on again when the bus reached Portland?"

Audrey put her hand on Truman's. "Truman," she said. "We have to talk about something."

"I don't get it," Truman went on. "Why would he travel blind like that? Why would he go all that way in the dark?"

"Truman, listen," Audrey said. But when Truman turned to her she took her hand away from his and looked across the table at George. George's eyes were closed. His fingers were folded together as if in prayer.

"George," Audrey said. "Please, I can't."

George opened his eyes.

"Tell him," Audrey said.

Truman looked back and forth between them. "Now just wait a minute," he said.

"I'm sorry," George said. "This is not easy for me."

Truman was staring at Audrey. "Hey," he said.

She pushed her empty glass back and forth. "We have to talk," she said.

He brought his face close to hers. "Do you think that just because I make a lot of money I don't have feelings?"

"We have to talk," she repeated.

"Indeed," George said.

The three of them sat there for a while. Then Truman said, "This takes the cake," and put his hat on. A few moments later they all got up and left the coffeehouse.

The waitress sat by herself at the bar, motionless except when she raised her head to blow smoke at the ceiling. Over by the door the Italians were throwing dice for toothpicks. "The Anvil Chorus" was playing on the jukebox. It was the first piece of classical music Charlie had heard often enough to get sick of, and he was sick of it now. He closed the magazine he'd been pretending to read, dropped it on the table, and went outside.

It was still foggy, and colder than before. Charlie's father had warned him about moving here in the middle of the summer. He had even quoted Mark Twain at Charlie, to the effect that the coldest winter Mark Twain ever endured was the summer he spent in San Francisco. This had been a particularly bad one—even the natives said so. In truth it was beginning to get to Charlie. But he had not admitted this to his father, any more than he had admitted that his job was wearing him out and paying him barely enough to keep alive on, or that the friends he wrote home about did not exist, or that the editors to whom he'd submitted his novel had sent it back without comment—all but one, who had scrawled in pencil across the title page: "Are you kidding?"

Charlie's room was on Broadway, at the crest of the hill. The hill was so steep they'd had to carve steps into the sidewalk and block the street with a cement wall because of the cars that had lost their brakes going down. Sometimes, at night, Charlie would sit on that wall and look out over the lights of North Beach and think of all the writers out there bent over their desks, steadily filling pages with well-chosen words. He thought of these writers gathering together in the small hours to drink wine, and read each other's work, and talk about the things that weighed on their hearts. These were the brilliant men and women, the deep conversations Charlie wrote home about.

He was close to giving up. He didn't even know how close to giving up he was, until he walked out of the coffeehouse that night and felt himself deciding that he would go on after all. He stood there and listened to the foghorn blowing out upon the bay. The sadness of that sound, the idea of himself stopping to hear it, the thickness of the fog all gave him pleasure.

Charlie heard violins behind him as the coffeehouse door opened; then it banged shut and the violins were gone. A deep voice said something in Italian. A higher voice answered, and the two voices floated away together down the street.

Charlie turned and started up the hill, picking his way past lampposts that glistened with running beads of water, past sweating walls and dim windows. A Chinese woman appeared beside him. She held before her a lobster that was waving its pincers back and forth as if conducting music. The woman hurried past and vanished. The hill began to steepen under Charlie's feet. He stopped to catch his breath, and listened again to the foghorn. He knew that somewhere out there a boat was making its way home in spite of the solemn warning, and as he walked on Charlie imagined himself kneeling in the prow of that boat, lamp in hand, intent on the light shining just before him. All distraction gone. Too watchful to be afraid. Tongue wetting the lips and eyes wide open, ready to call out in this shifting fog where at any moment anything might be revealed.

Hunktown

JOANN NOTICED that her daughter Patty had started parting her hair on the left, so that it fell over the right side of her forehead, hiding the scar from her recent car accident.

"That scar doesn't show, Mom," said Patty, when she caught Joann looking. Patty had the baby on her hip, and her little girl, Kristi, was on the floor fooling with the cat.

"Where's Cody?" Patty asked.

"Gone to Nashville. He got tired of waiting for that big shot he met in Paducah to follow up on his word, so he's gone down with Will Ed and them to make a record album on his own." Joann's husband, Cody Swann, was going to make a record album. She could hardly believe it. Cody had always wanted to make a record album.

"Is it one of those deals where you pay the studio?" Patty asked suspiciously.

"He pays five hundred dollars for the studio, and then he gets ten percent after they sell the first thousand."

"That's a rip-off," said Patty. "Don't he know that? I saw that on *60 Minutes*."

"Well, he got tired of waiting to be discovered. You know how he is."

The baby, Rodney, started to cry, and Patty stuck a pacifier in his mouth. She said, "The thing is, will they distribute the record? Them companies get rich making records for every little two-bit band that can hitchhike to Nashville. And then they don't distribute the records."

"Cody says he can sell them to all his fans around here."

"He could sell them at the store," Patty said. She worked at a discount chain store.

"He took off this morning in that van with the muffler dragging. He had it wired up underneath and tied with a rope to the door handle on the passenger side."

"That sounds just like Cody. For God's sake, Kristi, what are you doing to that cat?"

Kristi had the cat upside down between her knees. "I'm counting her milkers. She's got four milkers."

"That's a tomcat, hon," said Joann gently.

Joann was taking her daughter shopping. Patty, who had gotten a ride to Joann's, was depending on her mother for transportation until the insurance money came through on her car. She had totaled it when she ran into a blue Buick, driven by an old woman on her way to a white sale in town. Patty's head had smashed against the steering wheel, and her face had been so bruised that for a while it resembled a ripe persimmon blackened by frost.

With the children in the back seat, Joann drove Patty around town on her errands. Patty didn't fasten her seat belt. She had had two wrecks before she was eighteen, but this latest accident was not her fault. Cody said Patty's middle name was Trouble. In high school, she became pregnant and had to get married, but a hay bale fell on her and caused a miscarriage. After that, she had two babies, but then she got divorced. Patty had a habit of flirting with Cody and teasing her mother for marrying such a good-looking man. Cody had grown up in a section of town known as Hunktown because so many handsome guys used to live there. That part of town—a couple of streets between Kroger's and the high school—was still known as Hunktown. The public-housing project and the new health clinic were there now. Recently, a revival of pride in Hunktown had developed, as though it had been designated a historic area, and Cody had a Hunktown T-shirt. He wore cowboy outfits, and he hung his hats in a row on the scalloped trim of the china cabinet that Joann had antiqued.

Joann had known Cody since high school, but they had married only three years ago. After eighteen years of marriage to Joe Murphy, Joann found herself without a man — one of those women whose husbands suddenly leave them for someone younger. Last year, Phil Donahue had a show on that theme, and Joann remembered Phil saying something ironic like "It looks like you've got to keep tap-dancing in your negligee or the son-of-a-gun is going to leave you." Joann was too indignant to sit around and feel sorry for herself. After filing for divorce, she got a new hairdo and new clothes and went out on weekends with some women. One night, she went to a place across the county line that sold liquor. Cody Swann was there, playing a fancy red electric guitar and singing about fickle women and trucks and heartache. At intermission, they reminisced about high school. Cody was divorced, and he had two grown children, Joann had two teenagers still living at home, and Patty had already left. In retrospect, Joann realized how impulsive their marriage had been, but she had been happy with Cody until he got laid off from his job, four months ago. He'd worked at the Crosbee plant, which manufactured electrical parts. Now he was drinking too much, but he assured Joann he couldn't possibly become an alcoholic on beer. Their situation was awkward, because she had a good job at the post office, and she knew he didn't like to depend on her. He had thrown himself into rehearsing for his album with his friends Will Ed and L. J. and Jimmy. "What we really need is a studio," Cody kept saying impatiently. They had been playing at county fairs and civic events around western Kentucky off and on for years. Every year, Cody played at the International Banana Festival, in Fulton, and recently he had played for the Wal-

Mart grand opening and got a free toaster.

"Being out of work makes you lose your self-respect," Cody had told Joann matter-of-factly. "But I ain't going to let that happen to me. I've been fooling around too much. It's time to get serious about my singing."

"I don't want you to get your hopes up too much and then get disappointed," Joann said.

"Can't you imagine me with a television series? You could be on it with me. We'd play like we were Porter Wagoner and Dolly Parton. You could wear a big wig and balloons in your blouse."

"I can just see me — Miss Astor, in my plow shoes!" Joann said, squealing with laughter at the idea, playing along with Cody's dream.

Do you care if we drive out to that truck patch and pick a few turnip greens before I take you home?" Joann asked Patty. "It's on the way."

"You're the driver. Beggars can't be choosers." Patty rummaged around on the floor under the bucket seat and found Rodney's pacifier, peppered with tobacco and dirt. She wiped it on her jeans and jammed it into the baby's mouth.

On the CB, a woman suddenly said, "Hey, Tomcat, you lost something back here. Come in, Tomcat. Over." A spurt of static followed. The woman said, "Tomcat, it looks like a big old sack of feed. You better get in reverse."

"She's trying to get something started with those cute guys in that green pickup we passed," Patty said.

"Everybody's on the make," Joann said uneasily. She knew what that was like.

At the truck patch, Patty stood there awkwardly in her high heels, like a scarecrow planted in the dirt.

"Let me show you how to pick turnip greens," Joann said. "Gather them like this. Just break them off partway down the stem, and clutch them in your hand till you get a big wad. Then pack them down in the sack."

"They're fuzzy, and they sting my hands. Is this a turnip green or a weed?" Patty held up a leaf.

"That's mustard. Go ahead and pick it. Mustard's good." Joann flicked the greens off expertly. "Don't get down into the stalk," she said. "And they wilt down when they're cooked, so pack them real good."

Kristi was looking for bugs, and Rodney was asleep in the car. Joann bent over, grabbing the greens. Some of the turnips were large enough to pull, their bulbs showing aboveground like lavender pomanders. The okra plants in a row next to the turnip patch were as tall as corn, with yellow blossoms like roses. Where the blossoms had shriveled, the new okras thrust their points skyward. Joann felt the bright dizziness of the Indian-summer day, and she remembered many times when nothing had seemed important except picking turnip greens. She and Cody had lived on her parents' farm since her father died, two years before, but they had let it go. Cody wasn't a farmer. The field where her father used to grow turnips was wild now, spotted with burdock and thistles, and Cody was away in Nashville, seeking fame.

At a shed on the edge of the patch, Joann paid for the turnip greens and bought half a bushel of sweet potatoes from a black man in overalls, who was selling them from the back end of a pickup truck. The man measured the sweet potatoes in a half-bushel basket, then transferred them to grocery sacks. When he packed the sweet potatoes in the basket, he placed them so that their curves fit into one another, filling up the spaces. The man's carefulness was like Cody's when he was taping, recording a song over and over again. But Cody had tilled the garden last week in such a hurry that it looked as though cows had trampled the ground.

The man was saying, "When you get home with these, lay

them in a basket and don't stir them. The sweet will settle in them, but if you disturb them, it will go away. Use them off the top. Don't root around in them."

"I'll put them in the basement," Joann said, as he set the sacks into her trunk. She said to Patty, who was concentrating on a hangnail, "Sweet potatoes are hard to keep. They mold on you."

That evening, Joann discovered one of Cody's tapes that she had not heard before. On the tape, he sang a Webb Pierce song, "There Stands the Glass," that used to make her cry, the way Cody sang it so convincingly. When Cody sang "The Wild Side of Life" on the tape, Joann recalled Kitty Wells's answer to that song. "It wasn't God who made honky-tonk angels," Kitty Wells had insisted, blaming unfaithful men for every woman's heartbreak. Joann admired the way Kitty Wells sang the song so matter-of-factly, transcending her pain. A man wrote that song, Cody had told her. Joann wondered if he was being unfaithful in Nashville. She regarded the idea in a detached way, the way she would look at a cabbage at Kroger's.

Now Cody was singing an unfamiliar song. Joann rewound the tape and listened.

"I was born in a place they call Hunktown,
Good-lookin's my middle name—"

The song startled her. He had been talking about writing his own material, and he had started throwing around terms like "backup vocals" and "sound mixing." In this song, he sang along with himself to get a multiple-voice effect. The song was a lonesome tune about being a misfit. It sounded strangely insincere.

When Cody returned from Nashville, his voice bubbled along enthusiastically, like a toilet tank that ran until the handle was jiggled. He had been drinking. Joann had missed him, but she realized she hadn't missed his hat. It was the one with the pheasant feathers. He hung it on the china cabinet again. Cody was happy. In Nashville, he had eaten surf-and-turf, toured the Ryman Auditorium, and met a guy who had once been a sideman for Ernest Tubb.

"And here's the best part," said Cody, smacking Joann on the lips again. She got a taste of his mint-flavored snuff. "We got a job playing at a little bar in Nashville on weekends. It just came out of the blue. Jimmy can't do it, because his daddy's real bad off, but Will Ed and L.J. and me could go. Their wives already said they could."

"What makes you think I'll let you?" she said, teasing.

"You're going with me."

"But I've got too much to do." She set his boots on a carpet sample near the door to the porch. Cold air was coming through the crack around the facing. Cody had pieced part of the facing with a broken yardstick when he installed the door, but he had neglected to finish the job.

Cody said, "It's just a little bar with a little stage and this great guy that runs it. He's got a motel next to it and we can stay free. Hey, we can live it up in Nashville! We can watch Home Box Office and everything."

"How can I go? Late beans are coming in, and all them tomatoes."

"This is my big chance! Don't you think I sing good?"

"You're as good as anybody on the *Grand Ole Opry*."

"Well, there you go," he said confidently.

"Patty says those studio deals are rip-offs. She saw it on *60 Minutes*."

"I don't care. The most I can lose is five hundred dollars. And at least I'll have a record album. I'm going to frame the cover and put it in the den."

In bed, they lay curled together, like sweet potatoes. Joann listed to Cody describe how they had made the album, laying down separate tracks and mixing the sound.

Each little operation was done separately. They didn't just go into a studio and sing a song, Joann realized. They patched together layers of sound. She didn't mention the new song she had heard. She had put the tape back where she had found it. Now another of Cody's tapes was playing—"I'd Rather Die Young," a love song that seemed to have pointless suffering in it. Softly, Cody sang along with his taped voice. This was called a backup vocal, Joann reminded herself, trying to be very careful, taking one step at a time. Still, the idea of his singing with himself made her think of something self-indulgent and private, like masturbation. But country music was always like that, so personal.

"I'm glad you're home," she said, reaching for him.

"The muffler fell off about halfway home," Cody said with a sudden hoot of laughter that made the covers quiver. "But we didn't get caught. I don't know why, though. It's as loud as a hundred amplifiers."

"Hold still," Joann said. "You're just like a wiggle-worm in hot ashes."

Cody was trying on his new outfit for the show, and Joann had the sewing machine out, to alter the pants. The pants resembled suede and had fringe.

"They feel tight in the crotch," Cody said. "But they didn't have the next size."

"Are you going to tell me what you paid for them?"

"I didn't pay for them. I charged them at Penney's."

Joann turned the hem up and jerked it forward so that it fell against his boot. "Is that too short?" she asked.

"Just a little longer."

Joann pulled the hem down about a quarter-inch and pinned it. "Turn around," she said.

The pants were tan with dark-brown stitching. The vest was embroidered with butterflies. Cody turned around and around, examining himself in the long mirror.

"You look wonderful," she said.

He said, "We may get deeper in debt before it's over with, but one thing I've learned: You can't live with regret. You have to get on with your life. I know it's a big risk I'm taking, but I don't want to go around feeling sorry for myself because I've wasted so much time. And if I fail, at least I will have tried."

He sat on the bed and pulled his boots and then his pants off. The pants were too tight, but the seams were narrow, and there was no way Joann could let them out.

"You'll have to do something about that beer gut," she said.

The Bluebird Lounge looked as innocent as someone's kitchen: all new inside, with a country decor—old lanterns, gingham curtains, and a wagon wheel on the ceiling. It seemed odd to Joann that Cody had said he didn't want to live with regret, because his theme was country memories. He opened with "Walking the Floor Over You," then eased into "Your Cheatin' Heart," "The Wild Side of Life," and "I'd Rather Die Young." He didn't sing the new song she had heard on the tape, and she decided that he must be embarrassed by it. She liked his new Marty Robbins medley, a tribute to the late singer, though she had always detested the song "El Paso." In the pleasant atmosphere of the bar, Cody's voice sounded professional, more real there, somehow, than at home. Joann felt proud. She laughed when Will Ed and L.J. goofed around onstage, tripping over their electric cords and repeating things they had heard on *Hee Haw*. L.J. had been kidding Joann, saying, "You better come to Nashville with us to keep the girls from falling all over Cody." Now Joann noticed the women, in twos and threes, sitting close to the stage, and she remembered the time she went across the county line and heard Cody sing.

He still looked boyish, and he didn't have a single gray hair. She had cut his bangs too short, she realized now.

"They're really good," the cocktail waitress, Debbie, a slim, pretty woman in an embroidered cowboy shirt, said to Joann. "Most of the bands they get in here are so bad they really bum me out, but these guys are good."

"Cody just cut an album," Joann said proudly.

Debbie was friendly, and Joann felt comfortable with her, even though Debbie was only a little older than Patty. By the second night, Joann and Debbie were confiding in each other and trading notes on their hair. Joann's permanent was growing out strangely, and she was afraid getting a new permanent so soon would damage her hair, but Debbie got a permanent every three months and her hair stayed soft and manageable. In the restroom, Debbie fluffed her hair with her fingers and said, looking into the mirror, "I reckon I better put on some lipstick to keep the mortician away."

During the intermission, Debbie brought Joann a free tequila sunrise at her corner table. Cody was drinking beer at the bar with some musicians he had met.

"You've got a good-looking guy," Debbie said.

"He knows it, too," said Joann.

"He'd be blind if he didn't. It must be hard to be married to a guy like that."

"It wasn't so hard till he lost his job and got this notion that he has to get on the *Grand Ole Opry*."

"Well, he just might do it. He's good." Debbie told her about a man who had been in the bar once. He turned out to be a talent scout from a record company. "I wish I could remember his name," she said.

"I wish Cody would sing his Elvis songs," Joann said. "He can curl his lip exactly like Elvis, but he says he respects the memory of Elvis too much to do an Elvis act like everybody's doing. It would be exploitation."

"Cody sure is full of sad, lonesome songs," Debbie said.

"You can tell he's a guy who's been through a lot. I always study people's faces. I'm fascinated by human nature."

"He went through a bad divorce," Joann said. "But right now he's acting like a kid."

"Men are such little boys," Debbie said knowingly.

Joann saw Cody talking with the men. Their behavior was easygoing, full of laughter. Women were so intense together. Joann could feel Cody's jubilation all the way across the room. It showed in the energetic way he sang the mournful music of all the old hillbilly singers.

Debbie said, "Making music must make you feel free. If I could make music, I'd feel that life was one big jam session."

Coming home on Sunday was disorienting. The cat looked impatient with them. The weather was changing, and the flowers were dying. Joann had meant to take the potted plants into the basement for the winter. There had been a cold snap, but not a killing frost. The garden was still producing, languidly, after a spurt of growth during the last spell of warm weather. After work, during the week, Joann gathered in lima beans and squash and dozens of new green tomatoes. She picked handfuls of dried Kentucky Wonder pole beans to save for seed. Burrs clung to the cuffs of her jeans. Her father used to fight the burdock, knowing that one plant could soon take over a field.

Cody stayed indoors, listening to tapes and playing his guitar. He collected his unemployment check, but when someone called about a job opening, he didn't go. As she worked in the garden, Joann tried to take out her anger on the dying plants that she pulled from the soil. She felt she had to hurry. Fall weather always filled her with a sense of urgency.

Patty stopped by in her new Lynx. She had come out ahead on the insurance deal. Cody paraded around the car, admiring it, stroking the fenders.

"When's your album coming out, Cody?" Patty asked.

"Any day now."

"I asked at the store if they could get it, but they said it would have to be nationally distributed for them to carry it."

"Do you want a mess of lima beans, Patty?" Joann asked. "There's not enough for a canning, so I'll let you have them."

"No, this bunch won't eat any beans but jelly beans." Patty turned to Cody, who was peering under the hood of her car. "I told all the girls at work about your album, Cody. We can't wait to hear it. What's on it?"

"It's a surprise," he said, looking up. "They swore I'd have it by Christmas. The assistant manager of the studio said he thought it was going to be big. He told that to the Oak Ridge Boys and he was right."

"Wow," said Patty.

When Cody patted the pinch of snuff under his lip, she said, "I think snuff's kind of sexy."

Joann hauled the baby out of the car seat and bounced him playfully on her shoulder. "Who's precious?" she asked the baby.

In the van on the way to Nashville that Friday, they sang gospel songs, changing the words crazily. "Swing Low, Sweet Chariot" became "Sweet 'n Low, Mr. Coffee pot, perking for to hurry my heart." Cody drove, and Joann sat in the back, where she could manage the food. She passed out beer and the sandwiches she had made before work that morning. She had been looking forward to the weekend, hoping to talk things over with Debbie.

Will Ed sat in the back with Joann, complaining about his wife, who was taking an interior-decorating course by correspondence. "She could come with us, but instead she wants to stay home and rearrange the furniture. I'm afraid to go home in the dark. I don't know where to walk." He added with a laugh, "And I don't know *who* I might stumble over."

"Joyce wouldn't cheat on you," said Joann.

"What do you think all these songs we sing are about?" he asked.

At that moment, Cody was humming "Pop a Top," a song about a wandering wife. He reached back for another beer, and Joann pulled the tab off for him. Cody set the can between his legs and said, "Poor Joann here's afraid we're going to get corrupted. She thinks I ought to be home spreading manure and milking cows."

"Don't 'poor Joann' me. I can take care of myself."

Cody laughed. "If men weren't tied down by women, what do you reckon they'd do with themselves? If they didn't have kids, a house, installments to pay?"

"Men want to marry and have a home just as much as women do, or they wouldn't do it," Joann said.

"Tell him, Joann," said L.J.

"Listen to this," said Will Ed. "I asked Joyce what was for supper? And she says, '*I'm* having a hamburger. What are *you* going to have?' I mean you can't say a word now without 'em jumping on you."

"Y'all shut up," said Joann. "Let's sing another song. Let's sing 'The Old Rugged Cross.'"

"The old rugged cross" turned into "an old Chevrolet," a forlorn image, it seemed to Joann, like something of quality lost in the past. She imagined a handsome 1957 Chevrolet, its fins slashed by silver arrows, standing splendidly on top of a mountain.

"This is better than showing up at the plant with a lunch box!" Cody cried. "Ain't it, boys?" He blasted the horn twice at the empty highway and broke into joyous song.

At the Bluebird, Joann drank the tequila sunrises Debbie brought her. The drink was pretty, with an orange slice—a rising sun—on the rim of the glass. Between customers,

Debbie sat with Joann and they talked about life. Debbie knew a lot about human nature, though Joann wasn't sure Debbie was right about Cody being a man who suffered. "If he's suffering, it's because I'm bringing in the paycheck," she said. "But instead of looking for work, he's singing songs."

"He's going through the change," Debbie said. "Men go through it too. He's afraid he's missed out on life. I've seen a lot of guys like that."

"I don't understand what's happening to people, the way they can't hold together anymore," Joann said. "My daughter's divorced, and I think it's just now hitting me that I got divorced too. In my first marriage, I got shafted —eighteen years with a man, working my fingers to the bone, raising three kids—but I didn't make a federal case of it. I was lucky Cody came along. Cody says don't live with regret, but it's awful hard to look forward when there's so little you can depend on."

Debbie jumped up to get a draft beer for a man who signaled her. When she returned, she suddenly confessed to Joann, "I had my tubes tied—but I was such an idiot! And now I've met this new guy and he doesn't know. I think I'm serious about him, but I haven't got the heart to tell him what I did."

"When did you have it done?" Joann cried, horrified.

"Last spring." She lit a cigarette and exhaled smoke furiously. "You know why I got my tubes tied? Because I hate to be categorized. My ex-husband thought I had to have supper on the table at six on the dot, when he came home. I was working too, and I got home about five-thirty. I had to do all the shopping and cleaning and cooking. I hate it when people *assume* things like that—that I'm the one to make supper because I've got reproductive organs."

"I never thought of it that way exactly."

"I was going to add kids to those responsibilities? Like hell." Debbie punched holes in a cocktail napkin with her ballpoint pen. The napkin had jokes printed on it and she punched out the jokes. "It's the little things," she said. "I don't care about equal pay as much as I care about people judging me by the way I keep house. It's nobody's damn business how I keep house."

Joann had never heard of anything like what Debbie had done. She hadn't known a woman would go that far to make a point to a man. Later, Debbie said, "You don't know what problems are till you go through tubal litigation." Joann had a feeling that that was the wrong term, but she didn't want to mention it.

"I hate to see you so upset," Joann said. "What can I do?"

"Tell them to stop playing those lovesick songs. All these country songs are so stupid. They tell you to stand by your man, but then they say he's just going to use you somehow."

Joann thought she understood how Debbie felt about telling her new boyfriend what she had done. It seemed like a dreadful secret. Debbie had had her tubes tied rather than tell her husband in plain English to treat her better. The country songs were open and confessional, but in reality people kept things to themselves. The songs were an invasion of privacy. Debbie must have felt something like that about her housekeeping and her husband's demands. Debbie should have sung a song about it, instead of getting herself butchered, Joann thought. But maybe Debbie couldn't sing. Joann was getting drunk.

The next afternoon, at the motel, Cody said to Joann, "They want us to play five nights a week at the bar. They've guaranteed me six months." He was smiling and slamming things around happily. He had just brought in some Cokes and Big Macs. "Will Ed and L.J. have to stay home and work, but I can get some backup men from here, easy. We could get a little apartment down here and put the house up for sale."

"I don't want to sell Daddy's place." Joann's stomach was churning.

"Well, we ain't doing nothing with it."

"They say they're going to hire again at the plant in the spring," Joann said.

"To hell with the plant. I gave 'em nineteen years and six months of my life and they cut me off without a pension. Screw *them*."

Joann placed the Big Macs and Cokes on a tray. She and Cody sat on one of the two beds to eat. She nibbled at her hamburger. "You're telling me to quit my job," she said.

"You could find something in Nashville."

"And be a cocktail waitress like Debbie? No, thanks. That's a rough life. I like my job and I'm lucky to have it."

On TV, a preacher was yelling about reservations for heaven. Cody got up and flipped the dial, testing all the channels. "Just look how many TV channels we could get if we lived down here," he said.

"Don't do it, Joann," Debbie said flatly that evening.

"Cody and I haven't been together that long," Joann said. "Sometimes I feel I don't even know him. We're still in that stage where I ought to be giving him encouragement, the way you should do when you're starting out with somebody." She added, sarcastically, "Stand by your man."

"We're always caught in one cliché or another," Debbie said. "But you've got to think about yourself, Joann."

"I should give him more of a chance. He's got his heart set on this, and I'm being so contrary."

"But look what he's asking you to do, girl! Look what-all you've worked for. You've got your daddy's homeplace and that good job. You don't want to lose all that."

"We wouldn't come out ahead, after we pay off the mortgage. Maybe he wants to move to Nashville because there's ninety-nine TV stations to choose from. Well, the cable's coming down our road next year, and we'll have ten channels. That's enough television for anybody. They're bidding on the franchise now."

"I never watch television," Debbie said. "I can't stand watching stuff that's straight out of my own life."

At home, Cody was restless, full of nervous energy. He repaired some fences, as if getting the place ready to sell, but Joann hadn't agreed to anything. In the den one evening, after *Dynasty* had ended, Cody turned the sound down and said, "Let's talk, Jo." She waited while he opened a beer. He had been drinking beer after beer, methodically. "I've been thinking a lot about the way things are going, and I feel bad about how I used to treat my first wife, Charlene. I'm afraid I'm doing you the same way."

"You don't treat me bad," Joann said.

"I've taken advantage of you, letting you pay all the bills. I know I should get a job, but, damn it, there's got to be more to life than punching a time clock. I think I always expected a lot more out of life than most people. I used to be a real hell-raiser. I thought I could get away with anything because people always gave me things. All my life people gave me things."

"What things?" Joann was sitting on the couch and Cody was in the easy chair. The only light came from the television.

"In grade school, I'd get more Valentines than anybody, and the Valentines would have candy in them, little hearts with messages like 'Be Mine' and 'Cutie' and things like that. When I graduated from high school, all the storekeepers in town gave me stuff and took me in their back rooms and gave me whiskey. I had my first drink in the pharmacy in the back of the Rexall. I just breezed through life, letting people give me things, and it didn't dawn on me for a long time that people wanted something back. They expected something from me and I never gave it to them. I didn't live up to their expectations. Somehow, I want to give something back."

"People always admired you, Cody. You're so good-natured. Isn't that giving something?"

Cody belched loudly and laughed. "When I was about twelve, a man gave me five dollars to jack him off in the alley behind the old A&P."

"Did you do it?"

"Yep. And I didn't think a thing about it. I just did it. Five bucks was five bucks."

"Well, what do you owe *him*?" Joann said sharply.

"Nothing, I reckon, but the point is, I did a lot of stuff that wasn't right. Charlene was always thumping the Bible and hauling me off to church. I couldn't live with that. I treated her like dirt, the way I cheated on her. I always wanted what was free and available. It was what I was used to. I had a chance once, about fifteen years ago, to play in a little bar in Nashville, but the kids were little, and Charlene didn't want me to go. I've regretted that to this day. Don't you see why this chance means so much to me? I'm trying to *give* something of myself, instead of always taking. Just go along with me, Joann. Take this one risk with me."

"What can I say when you put it that way?"

"A person has to follow his dream."

"That sounds like some Elvis song," she said, sounding unexpectedly sarcastic. She was thinking of Elvis's last few years, when he got fat and corrupted. She rearranged some pillows on the couch. The weather news was on TV. The radar was showing rain in their area. Slowly, her eyes on the flashing lines of the radar map, she said, "What you want to do is be in the spotlight so people can adore you. That's the same thing as taking what's free."

"That's not true. Maybe you think it's easy to be in the spotlight. But it's not. Look what happened to Elvis."

"You're not Elvis. And selling the place is too extreme. Things can't be all one way or the other. There has to be

some of both. That's what life is, when it's any good." Joann
felt drained, as though she had just had to figure out all of
life, like doing a complicated math problem in her head.

Cody turned the TV off and the light vanished. In the
dark, he said, "I cheated on Charlene, but I never cheated
on you."

"I never said you did."

"But you expect it," he said.

Patty came over to ask Joann to keep the kids that weekend. She had a new boyfriend who was taking her to St.
Louis.

"If I can take 'em to Nashville," Joann told Patty. "I have
to go along to keep the girls away from Cody." She looked
meaningfully at Cody.

It was meant to be a casual, teasing remark, she thought,
but it didn't come out that way. Cody glared at her, looking
hurt.

"The kids will be in the way," he said. "You can't take
them to the Bluebird Lounge."

"We'll stay in the motel room," Joann said. "I wanted to
watch *On Golden Pond* on HBO anyway. Nashville has so
much more to offer. Remember?"

She realized that taking the children to Nashville was a
bad idea, but she felt she had to go with Cody. She didn't
know what might happen. She hoped that having the kids
along would make her and Cody feel they had a family to be
responsible for. Besides, Patty was neglecting the kids.
Joann had kept them three nights in a row last week while
Patty went out with her new boyfriend.

In the van on the way down, Rodney cried because he
was teething, and L.J. gave him a piece of rawhide to chew
on. Kristi played with a bucket of plastic toys. Will Ed practiced the middle eight of a new song they had learned. It
seemed pointless to Joann, since Cody planned to dump

Will Ed and L.J. from his act. Will Ed played the passage over and over on his guitar, until Kristi screamed, "Shut up!" Cody said little. L.J. was driving, because Joann didn't want Cody to drive and drink beer, with the children along.

Daylight Savings Time had ended and the dark came early. The bright lights at the edge of Nashville reminded Joann of how soon Christmas was.

She liked being alone in the motel room with the kids. It made her think of when she'd had small children and her first husband had worked a night shift. She had always tried to be quiet around sleeping children, but nowadays children had more tolerance for noise. The TV didn't bother them. She sat in bed, propped against pillows. The children were asleep. In the large mirror facing the bed, she could see herself, watching TV, with the sleeping bundles beside her. Joann felt expectant, as if some easy answers were waiting for her—from the movie, from the innocence of the children.

Suddenly Kristi sat straight up and shouted, "Where's Mommy?"

"Hush, Kristi! Mommy's gone to St. Louis. We'll see her Sunday."

Kristi hurled herself out of bed and ran around the room. She looked in the closet and in the bathroom. Then she began to shriek. Joann grabbed her and whispered, "Shush, you'll wake up your little brother!"

Kristi wiggled away from her and looked under the bed, but the bed was boxed-in—a brilliant construction, Joann thought, so far as cleaning was concerned. Kristi bumped into a chair and fell down. She began bawling. Rodney stirred, and then he started to cry. Joann huddled both children in the center of the bed and began singing to them. She couldn't think of anything to sing except the Kitty Wells song about honky-tonk angels. The song was an absurd one to sing to kids, but she sang it anyway. It was her life. She sang it like an innocent bystander, angry that that was the way women were, that they looked on approvingly while some man went out and either did something big or made a fool of himself trying.

When Cody came in later, she had fallen asleep with the children. She woke up and glanced at the travel alarm. It was three. The TV was still on. Cody was missing the Burt Reynolds movie he had wanted to watch. He stumbled into the bathroom and then fell into the other bed with all his clothes on.

"I was rehearsing with those new guys," he said. "And then we went out to eat something." Joann heard his boots fall to the floor, and he said, "I called home around ten-thirty, between shows, to wish Mama a happy birthday, and she told me Daddy's in the Memphis hospital."

"Oh, what's wrong?" Joann sat up and pulled her pillow behind her. Cody's father, who was almost seventy-five, had always bragged about never being sick.

"It's cancer. He had some tests done. They never told me anything." Cody flung his shirt to the foot of the bed. "Lung cancer comes on sudden. They're going to operate next week."

"I was *so* afraid of that," Joann said. "The way he smoked."

Cody turned to face her across the aisle between the two beds. He reached over and searched for her hand. "I'll have to go to Memphis tomorrow night after the show. Mama's going down tomorrow."

Rodney squirmed beside Joann, and she pulled the covers around his shoulders. Then she crept into bed with Cody and lay close to him while he went on talking in a tone of disbelief about his father. "It makes me mad that I forgot it was Mama's birthday. I thought of it during the first show, when I was singing 'Blue Eyes Crying in the Rain.' I don't know how come me to think of it then."

"Do you want me to go to Memphis with you?"

"No. That's all right. You have to get the kids home. I'll

take the bus and then come back here for the show Tuesday." Cody drew her near him. "Were you going to come back with me?"

"I've been thinking about that. I don't want to quit my job or sell Daddy's place. That would be crazy."

"Sometimes it's good to act a little crazy."

"No. We have to reason things out, so we don't ruin anything between us." She was half-whispering, trying not to wake the children, and her voice trembled as though she were having a chill. "I think you should come down here by yourself first and see how it works out."

"What if my album's a big hit and we make a million dollars?" His eyes were on the TV. Burt Reynolds was speeding down an interstate.

"That would be different."

"Would you move to Nashville if I got on the *Grand Old Opry*?"

"Yes."

"Is that a promise?"

"Yes."

On Monday, Cody was still in Memphis. The operation was the next day, and Joann took off from work early in order to go down to be with Cody and his parents. She was ready to leave the house when the delivery truck brought the shipment of record albums. The driver brought two boxes, marked "1 of 3" and "2 of 3."

"I'll bring the third box tomorrow," the driver said. "We're not allowed to bring three at once."

"Why's that?" Joann asked, shivering in the open doorway to the porch.

"They want to keep us moving."

"Well, I don't understand that one bit."

Joann shoved the boxes across the threshold and closed the door. With a butcher knife, she ripped open one of the boxes and slipped out a record album. On the cover was a photograph of Cody and Will Ed and L.J. and Jimmy, sitting on a bench. Above them, the title of the album was a red-and-blue neon sign: HUNKTOWN. Cody and his friends were all wearing Hunktown T-shirts, cowboy boots, and cowboy hats. They had a casual, slouchy look, like the group called Alabama. It was a terrible picture. Looking at her husband, Joann thought no one would say he was really handsome. She held the cover up to the glass door to get a better light on his face. He looked old. His expression seemed serious and unforgiving, as though he expected the world to be ready for him, as though this were his revenge, not his gift. The face was now on a thousand albums.

But the picture was not really Cody at all, she thought. It was only his wild side, not the part she loved. Seeing it was something like identifying a dead body: it was so unfamiliar that death was somehow acceptable. She had to laugh. Cody had meant the album to be a surprise, but he would be surprised to see how he looked.

Joann heard a noise outside. She touched her nose to the door glass and left a smudge. On the porch, the impatiens in the hanging basket had died in the recent freeze. She had forgotten to bring the plant inside. Now she watched it sway and twist in a little whirl of wind.